D0384797

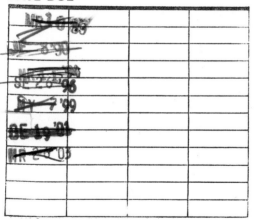

BORN
FREE

BORN FREE

A Lioness of Two Worlds

JOY ADAMSON

P A N T H E O N   B O O K S ,   N E W   Y O R K

ACKNOWLEDGMENTS

In writing the story of Elsa, I have made much use of my
husband's records, as well as including his letters in the
last chapter, and I would like to say that it is therefore
partly his book as well as mine.

There are several other people to whom it also owes
much: Lord William Percy, who has written the Preface,
and honored Elsa with his friendship; Captain Charles Pitman, the former Game Warden of Uganda, who has contributed the Foreword and given me valuable information;
Cecil Webb, formerly Curator of Mammals at Regent's
Park Zoo, and Director of Dublin Zoo, who has helped me
with the revision of the text; Dr. E. G. Appelman, Director
of Blydorp, who checked certain zoological data. I would
also like to thank Mrs. Robert Atkinson, and Mr. Adrian
House for taking such a personal interest in the produc-
tion of the book. But I owe most to Mrs. George Villiers,
without whose help and advice, particularly in regard to
the collation of the material, this record of Elsa's life
would never have appeared in its present form.

J. A.

Originally published in Great Britain by William Collins
Sons & Co. Ltd., and in the United States by Pantheon
Books, a division of Random House, Inc., in 1960.
Library of Congress Cataloging-in-Publication Data

Adamson, Joy.
   Born free, a lioness of two worlds.
   Sequel: Living free.
   1. Elsa (Lion) 2. Lions—Kenya—Behavior.
3. Lions—Kenya—Biography. 4. Mammals—Kenya—
Behavior. I. Title.
QL737.C23A178 1987   599.74'428   86-42972
ISBN 0-394-56141-4
ISBN 0-394-74635-X (pbk.)

Manufactured in the United States of America
First Pantheon Paperback Edition

Contents

Then the chief captain came, and said unto him,
Tell me, art thou a Roman?
He said, Yea.
And the chief captain answered,
With a great sum obtained I this freedom.
And Paul said, But I was free born.

Acts 22:27, 28

Foreword to the New Edition

IN 1956, George Adamson, a game warden in Kenya's Northern Frontier Province, was tracking a man-eating male lion when he was charged by a lioness. After shooting her, he discovered that she was lactating; she had been protecting her three tiny cubs. George took the orphaned litter home. Two cubs ultimately went to a zoo, but the third and smallest, named Elsa, was raised by George and his wife, Joy, from cuddly cub to sleek lioness. Determined not to deny her her natural heritage, the Adamsons returned Elsa to a life of freedom. They taught her to hunt and to kill, and they permitted her to roam the arid bush country at night, where she met and ultimately mated with wild lions. Even after she gave birth to three cubs in late 1959, Elsa retained an affectionate contact with her foster parents. As George wrote: "She is always very pleased to see me and obviously does not like to see me leave her, but if I were to stay away for good, I do not think it would upset her life very much." Elsa was truly a lioness of two worlds.

Born Free, the first of a trilogy, ends with the birth of Elsa's cubs. *Living Free* continues the saga. The cubs—Gopa, Little Elsa, and Jespah—joined their mother on visits to the Adamson's camp, where they romped among the tents. But when the cubs were a year old, Elsa died of babesia, a blood parasite, after spending her last hours with George in his tent, as if seeking the one world that would mourn her passing. After her death the cubs became wild, attacking domestic herds of goats instead of coming to the camp for meals. Banished by the government, they were offered refuge in Tanzania's vast Serengeti National Park. *Forever Free* describes Elsa's offspring in their new home, where, fully integrated into the wild, they soon lost contact with the Adamsons.

Born Free recounts Elsa's life so lovingly and has such evocative photographs that it has become an animal classic. Yet a reader's response to the book somehow transcends the story itself. After all, others have chronicled the return of animals to the wild. There is, of course, the romance of a game warden's existence, controlling marauding elephants, protecting animals from poachers. But above all, there is the lion itself. When humans observe an animal, they mainly see the fiction they have created for it. To humankind the lion is not just an animal but something vital and mysterious, the King of Beasts, the companion of royalty, a creature before whose thundering roar all living things quake with fear. Visitors to Africa's national parks seek the lion above all, vicariously exulting in the animal's strength from the safety of a vehicle. Even to see a lion sprawled languidly in the shade of an acacia tree is to sense the power of nature. In addition, every visitor carries away special memories of the cats. I spent over three years in the Serengeti studying lions, and remember the heavy tread of males on the wind-swept plains at night, and the menacing growls of a pride on a kill, the air heavy with the odor of blood and stomach contents as the animals bolted their food with a naked emotion almost foreign to human experience.

The Adamsons gave us another and a new image of the lion, an immensely appealing one of a playful, devoted, kindly, and even vulnerable creature; they gave us truths about the species that cannot be found in a biologist's notebook, hunter's tale, or tourist's account. We are at a turning point in our relationship with animals, and *Born Free* is one of the finest illustrations of this. Even the lion, immensely powerful and reputedly fierce, may establish emotional ties and a lasting bond with humans based on empathy and friendship. Elsa, like others animals, was not just an anonymous member of a species but an individual with her own foibles, aspirations, and sensitivities. Secure yet free, her individuality had a chance to blossom. By being on such intimate terms with Elsa and her cubs, the Adamsons came to know lions as individuals better than anyone I have met. In the Serengeti they told me of subtle gestures and sounds I had overlooked; they had entered the lion's world in a way that mere field observers cannot.

The Adamsons loved Elsa and her offspring. I first met Joy in 1966 when she revisited the Serengeti. Although five years had passed since the cubs had last been seen, she was still passionately concerned over their fate.

6

Unfortunately, I could only say that neither I nor anyone else had knowingly met them. Those who have raised a lion can well understand such devotion. Once, for several months, my wife Kay and I reared a cub that I had found abandoned and near death beside a wildebeest carcass. The cub soon became a full family member, friendly without fawning, without ever losing his dignity or subverting the independence of a wild animal. To have a lion firmly but gently rub its cheek against yours in greeting is to lose your heart to the species. In spite of the close bond that can exist between humans and lions, the cats are, in Henry Beston's words, "not brethren, they are not underlings; they are other nations caught with ourselves in the net of life and time, fellow prisoners of the splendor and travail of the earth." *Born Free* shows that we can to some extent overcome this cross-cultural barrier. And by doing so, we strengthen our feelings of belonging to the natural world.

Elsa changed the Adamsons; she gave their lives new direction. Together they dedicated themselves fully to rehabilitating lions, leopards, and cheetahs. At her death in 1980, Joy left an unequalled legacy of devotion to the big cats. Books and a movie made Elsa not only an international celebrity but also a force for conservation in that she helped create a new consciousness on behalf of Africa's wildlife. The Elsa Appeal, a conservation fund, was established by Joy in her name. In their book *Born Free*, pen and camera became a potent weapon on behalf of lions, and the Adamsons made Elsa and her kind an enduring presence. It is up to all of us to continue what they began, to make certain that the lion will survive, a symbol of all that is wild and free.

In these destructive times, with one ecological disaster following upon another, *Born Free* is an idyll, taking us into a world where animals and humankind live together in harmony. It affords us a view of the Peaceable Kingdom that we abandoned long ago; it is a reminder of how things were and how they could have been.

George B. Schaller

New York   Director of Wildlife Conservation International,
January 1987   New York Zoological Society

Preface

WHETHER fact or fiction lies at the root of tales which credit the Assyrians with having trained lions as cheetahs, greyhounds, or retrievers are today trained to hunt in co-operation with man, the Adamsons can certainly claim to be the first for several thousand years to have made an approach to achieving that result with a lioness—and that, *not* by any deliberate attempt to do so, but merely by allowing the animal to grow up in their company and *never* allowing her nature to be subjected to the strains of being confined in any way.

The history of the lioness Elsa, reared from earliest infancy to three years old and finally returned to a wild life, forms a unique and illuminating study in animal psychology—a subject to which the last half-century has seen a wholly new approach. Partly, no doubt, in revolt against the tendency of nineteenth-century writers to attribute to animals anthropomorphic qualities of intelligence, sentiment, and emotion, the twentieth century has seen the development of a school of thought according to which the springs of animal behavior are to be sought in terms of "conditioned reflexes," "release mechanisms," and the rest of a wholly new vocabulary which is regarded as the gateway to a clearer understanding of animal psychology. To another way of thinking, which cannot reconcile that mechanical conception with the diverse character, intelligence, and capabilities exhibited by different individuals of the same species, that gateway to understanding seems as far removed from truth as the anthropomorphism of a previous generation, and more apt to raise a further barrier to a sympathetic understanding of animal behavior than a revelation of it.

To whatever way of thinking the reader of Elsa's history may lean, it provides a record of absorbing interest depicting the gradual development of a controlled character which few would have credited as possible in the case of an animal potentially as dangerous as any in the world. That such a creature when in a highly excited state, with her blood up after a long struggle with a bull buffalo, and while still on top of it, should have permitted a man to walk up to her and cut the dying beast's throat to satisfy his religious scruples, and then lend her assistance in pulling the carcass out of a river, is an astonishing tribute no less to her intelligence than to her self-control.

If the most fanciful author of animal stories of the nineteenth century had drawn the imaginary character of a lioness acting in that manner it would assuredly have been ridiculed as altogether "out of character" and too improbable to carry conviction—and yet Elsa's record shows that it is no more than sober fact.

If in her development Elsa has made her own commentary both on the "anthropomorphism" of the nineteenth century and on the "science" of the twentieth, she has not lived in vain.

WILLIAM PERCY

Priestess and lion, Nineveh, 7th century B.C.

Foreword

To be invited to write a Foreword to Joy Adamson's fascinating story of Elsa, the lioness who was never "treated with either force or frustration," is indeed an honor and a privilege.

Vividly describing a most remarkable, probably unique, man-animal relationship, it well illustrates how the truth can be stranger than fiction.

The author and her husband, George, by the exercise of inexhaustible patience, cultivated so strong a bond of sympathy with the tiny cub that they were able to retain not only her friendship but her affectionate devotion when, long after reaching maturity, she became a full-grown, free-roaming lioness, and when one cuff from her mighty paw could mean a broken neck.

Despite manifestations of her latent inherent savagery, Elsa never lost—and I believe never will lose—that perfect trust and confidence in her human "parents" whom she regards with a peculiar devotion, a devotion which she would never have accorded her own kind. Thus it was that, when in the best interests of both it became advisable to return Elsa to the wild whence she had originally come, she accepted with equanimity and a pathetic dignity a situation which evidently puzzled her and, above all, she displayed no resentment.

But there is pathos in George's letters about his subsequent visits to Elsa's domain: she never failed to turn up to greet him, but he invariably wrote that there was no indication that she had joined up with a wild mate or pride. She had often associated with her feral congeners, but to join up with any of them permanently seemed to her to be a contingency to be avoided. Had her intimate association with the human race created too great a gulf between herself and the wild one, which could never be bridged? Was she an integral part of those she has so long loved and trusted? Many animals are subject to man, but Elsa is not; she was free born, never subject, developed a passionate devotion, and became an equal.

But, for a solution of this problem let us turn to the Envoi. Elsa is no longer dependent on her foster parents; at long last she has found a mate and her story moves toward a happy natural ending. So neither side has broken faith, and the Adamsons have eventually achieved what they set out to do. Elsa once again is of the wild. Long may she enjoy her natural existence.

We owe a debt of gratitude to Joy Adamson for a factual, vivid portrayal of the many aspects of this strange relationship which has lasted for four years. Some of the carefully compiled observations are of considerable scientific value: some have confounded certain of my own impressions of leonine behavior. May Elsa be spared for many years to add yet further to the incredible store of knowledge to which she has already so freely contributed.

George Adamson is the Senior Game Warden in an East African Game Department. His duties are primarily to preserve the wild life so long as it is not in direct conflict with man and his works. In consequence he is also charged with the control of wild life, and when necessary he may have to destroy dangerous and destructive wild animals such as lion and elephant, and so it was that Elsa was acquired. The area under him, mainly uninhabited, covers tens of thousands of square miles, and this he has to police, with a hopelessly inadequate force of Africans, in order to detect and prevent the poaching which is rife. This tale in its telling gives a general idea of his functions and of the manifold difficulties of his task, complicated as they inevitably were when he was accompanied by a full-grown lioness! Those were indeed astonishing journeys.

I conclude with the fervent hope that there may long be in this harsh world such human and kindly folk as Joy and George Adamson to take pity on the waifs of the wild.

C. R. S. PITMAN
Formerly Game Warden,
Uganda Protectorate

12 Chelsea Embankment,
London, S.W.3

BORN
FREE

Cub Life

F o r many years my home has been in the Northern Frontier Province of Kenya, that vast stretch of semiarid thornbush, covering some hundred and twenty thousand square miles, which extends from Mount Kenya to the Abyssinian border.

Civilization has made little impact on this part of Africa; there are no settlers; the local tribes live very much as their forefathers did, and the place abounds in wild life of every description.

My husband, George, is Senior Game Warden of this huge territory, and our home is on the southern border of the Province, near Isiolo, a small township of about thirty Whites, all of whom are government officials engaged in the task of administering the territory.

George has many duties, such as enforcing the Game Laws, preventing poaching, and dealing with dangerous animals that have molested the tribesmen. His work causes him to travel over tremendous distances; these journeys we call safaris. Whenever it is possible I accompany my husband on such trips, and in this way I have had unique opportunities of coming to grips with this wild, unchanged land, where life is tough and nature asserts her own laws.

This story has its beginning on one of these safaris. A Boran tribesman had been killed by a man-eating lion. It was reported to George that this animal, accompanied by two lionesses, was living in some near-by hills, and so it became his duty to track them down. This was why we were camping far to the north of Isiolo among the Boran tribesmen.

Early on the morning of the first of February, 1956, I found myself in camp alone with Pati, a rock hyrax who had been living with us as a pet for six and a half years. She looked like a marmot or a guinea pig, though zoologists will have it that on account of the bone structure of its feet and teeth, the hyrax is most nearly related to rhinos and elephants.

Pati snuggled her soft fur against my neck and from this safe position watched all that went on. The country around us was dry with outcrops of granite and only sparse vegetation; all the same there were animals to be seen, for there were plenty of gerenuk and other gazelles, creatures that have adapted themselves to these dry conditions and rarely, if ever, drink.

Suddenly I heard the vibrations of a car; this could only mean that George was returning much earlier than expected. Soon our Land Rover broke through the thornbush and stopped near our tents, and I heard George shout: "Joy, where are you? Quick, I have something for you. . . ."

I rushed out with Pati on my shoulder and saw the skin of a lion. But before I could ask about the hunt, George pointed to the back of the car. There were three lion cubs, tiny balls of spotted fur, each trying to hide its face from everything that went on. They were only a few days old and their eyes were still covered with a bluish film. They could hardly crawl; nevertheless they tried to creep away. I took them on my lap to comfort them, while George, who was most distressed, told me what had happened. Toward dawn he and another Game Warden, Ken, had been guided near to the place where the man-eater was said to lie up. When first light broke they were charged by a lioness who rushed out from behind some rocks. Though they had no wish to kill her, she was very close and the way back was hazardous, so George signalled to Ken to shoot; he hit and wounded her. The lioness disappeared, and when they went forward they found a heavy trail of blood leading upward. Cautiously, step by step, they went over the crest of the hill till they came to a huge flat rock. George climbed onto it to get a better view, while Ken skirted around below. Then he saw Ken peer under the rock, pause, raise his rifle, and fire both barrels. There was a growl; the lioness appeared and came straight at Ken. George could not shoot, for Ken was in his line of fire; fortunately, a Game Scout who was in a more favorable position fired his rifle and caused the animal to swerve; then George was able to kill her. She was a big lioness in the prime of life, her teats swollen with milk. It was only when he saw this that George realized why she had been so angry and faced them so courageously. Then he blamed himself for not having recognized earlier that her behavior showed that she was defending her litter.

Now he ordered a search to be made for the cubs; presently he and Ken heard slight sounds coming out of a crack in the rock face. They put their arms down the crevice as far as they could reach; loud infantile growls and snarls greeted this unsuccessful maneuver. Next they cut a long hooked stick and after a lot of probing managed to drag the cubs out; they could not have been more than two or three days old. They were carried to the car, where the two biggest growled and spat during the whole of the journey back to camp. The third and smallest, however, offered no resistance and seemed quite unconcerned. Now the three cubs lay in my lap, and how could I resist making a fuss of them?

To my amazement Pati, who was usually very jealous of any rival, soon came to nestle among them, and obviously accepted them as desirable companions. From that day onward, the four became inseparable. During these early days Pati was the biggest of the company and also, being six years old, was very dignified compared with the clumsy little velvet bags who couldn't walk without losing their balance.

It was two days before the cubs accepted their first milk. Until then, whatever trick I tried to make them swallow diluted unsweetened canned milk only resulted in their pulling up their tiny noses and protesting: "ng-ng, ng-ng," very much as we did as children, before we had learned better manners and been taught to say, "No, thank you."

Once they had accepted the milk, they could not get enough of it, and every two hours I had to warm it and clean the flexible rubber tube, which we had taken from the wireless set to serve as a teat until we were able to get a proper baby's bottle. We had sent at once to the nearest African market, which was about fifty miles away, not only for the teat but also for cod-liver oil, glucose, and cases of unsweetened milk and had at the same time sent an S.O.S. to the District Commissioner at Isiolo, about a hundred and fifty miles away, announcing the arrival there within a fortnight of Three Royal Babies, asking him to be good enough to have a comfortable wooden home made in time for our return.

Within a few days the cubs had settled down and were everybody's pets. Pati, their most conscientious self-appointed nanny, remained in charge; she was devoted to them, and never minded being pulled and trodden on by the three fast-growing little bullies. All the cubs were females. Even at this age each had a definite character. The "Big

Pati, the self-appointed nanny

The cubs, seven weeks old

One" had a benevolent superiority and was generous toward the others. The second was a clown, always laughing and spanking her milk bottle with both her front paws as she drank, her eyes closed in bliss. I named her Lustica, which means the "Jolly One."

The third cub was the weakling in size, but the pluckiest in spirit. She pioneered all around, and was always sent by the others to reconnoiter when something looked suspicious to them. I called her Elsa, because she reminded me of someone of that name.

In the natural course of events Elsa would probably have been the throw-out of the pride.[1] The average number of cubs in a litter is four, of which one usually dies soon after birth and another is often too weak to be reared. It is for this reason that one usually sees only two cubs with a lioness. Their mother looks after them till they are

[1] A "pride" is a loose term used to describe the association of more than two lions. It may consist of one or more families living together with some adults, or of a number of adults living together for the purpose of hunting in combination, in contradistinction to a pair of lions or a solitary lion.

two years old. For the first year she provides their food; she regurgitates it, thus making it acceptable to them. During the second year the cubs are allowed to take part in the hunting, but they get severely disciplined if they lose their self-control. Since at this time they are unable to kill on their own, they have to rely for their food on what may be left over from a kill by the full-grown lions of the pride. Often very little remains for them, so they are usually in a bad, scruffy condition at this age. Sometimes they can't bear the hunger; then either they break through the line of gorging adults and are likely to be killed, or they leave the pride, in small groups, and, because they do not yet know how to kill properly, often run into trouble. Nature's law is harsh, and lions have to learn the hard way from the beginning.

The quartet—Pati and the three cubs—spent most of the day in the tent under my camp bed; this evidently seemed to them a safe place and the nearest thing they could find to their natural nursery. They were by nature house-trained and always took great care to reach the sand outside. There were a few accidents during the first days, but afterward, on the rare occasions when a little pool disgraced their home, they miaowed and made comical grimaces of disgust. In every way they were wonderfully clean and had no smell except for a very pleasant one like honey—or was it cod-liver oil? Their tongues were already as rough as sandpaper; as they grew older we could feel them, even through our khaki clothes, when they licked us.

When, after two weeks, we returned to Isiolo, our Royal Babies had a palace awaiting them, everyone came to see them, and they received a royal welcome. They loved Europeans and especially small children but had a marked dislike of Africans; the only exception was a young Somali, called Nuru. He was our garden boy; now we appointed him guardian and lion-keeper in chief. The post pleased him, for it raised his social status; it also meant that when the cubs got tired of romping all over the house and its surroundings and preferred to sleep under some shady bush, he was able to sit near them for long hours, watching to see that no snakes or baboons molested them.

For twelve weeks we kept them on a diet of unsweetened milk mixed with cod-liver oil, glucose, bone-meal, and a little salt. Soon they showed us that they required only three-hourly feeds, and then gradually the intervals became longer.

By now their eyes were fully opened, but they could not yet judge distances and often missed their target. To help them over this difficulty we gave them rubber balls and old inner tubes to play with—the latter were perfect for tug-of-war games. Indeed, anything made of rubber, or that was soft and flexible, fascinated them. They would try to take the inner tube from each other, the attacker rolling sideways onto the possessor, pressing her weight between the end of the tube and its owner. If no success was achieved by this method, the rivals would simply pull with all their might. Then, when the battle had been won, the victor would parade with the trophy in front of the others and provoke an attack. If this invitation was ignored, the rubber would be placed in front of their noses, while the owner pretended to be unaware that it might be stolen from her.

Elsa asleep

The final stages of a stalk

Surprise was the most important element in all their games. They stalked each other—and us—from the earliest age and knew by instinct how to do it properly.

They always attacked from the rear; keeping under cover, they crouched, then crept slowly toward the unsuspecting victim until the final rush was made at flying speed and resulted in the attacker's landing with all her weight on the back of her quarry, throwing it to the ground. When we were the object of such an attack we always pretended to be unaware of what was going on; obligingly we crouched down and looked the other way until the final onslaught took place. This delighted the cubs.

Pati always wanted to be in the game, though, as the cubs were soon three times her size, she took good care to keep out of the way of heavy spankings and to avoid being squashed by her charges. In all other circumstances she retained her authority by sheer character; if the cubs became too aggressive she put them in their places by just turning around and facing them. I admired her spirit, for, small as she was, it needed a lot of courage to convince them of her fearlessness; the more so that her only defenses were her sharp teeth, quick reactions, intelligence, and pluck.

She had come to us when she was newly born, and had entirely adapted her life to ours. Unlike her cousin the tree hyrax, she was not a nocturnal animal, and at night she would sleep around my neck like a fur. She was a vegetarian but had a craving for alcohol, and for the strongest spirits at that; whenever the opportunity arose she would pull the bottle over, extract the cork, and swig the liquor. As this was very bad for Pati's health, not to mention her morale, we took every precaution to prevent any indulgence in whisky or gin.

Pati keeps out of reach (above & below)

A cub at four months

Her excretory habits were peculiar. Rock hyraxes always use the same place, by preference the edge of a rock; at home Pati invariably perched herself on the rim of the lavatory seat, and thus situated presented a comical sight. On safari where no such refinements were provided for her, she was completely bewildered, so we had eventually to rig up a small lavatory for her.

I never found a flea or a tick on her, so at first I was puzzled by her habit of constantly scratching herself. She had round toenails, like those of a miniature rhino, on her well-padded feet; four toes in front and three behind. On the inner toe of her hind legs there was a claw known as the grooming claw. With this she used to keep her fur sleek and her care for her coat explained her constant scratchings.

Pati had no visible tail; she had a gland along the middle of her spine, which was visible as a white patch in her otherwise brindled-gray fur. This gland discharged a secretion and the hair around it used to rise when she became excited by pleasure or alarm. As the cubs grew larger her hair stood up all too frequently owing to the fear which their playful but rough antics caused her. Indeed, had she not always been quick to seek refuge on a window sill, a ladder, or some other high object, she would often have been in danger of being mistaken by them for a rubber ball. Until the cubs came Pati had always been number one among our pets. So I was very touched that she should continue to love the little rascals even though they diverted our visitors' attention from herself.

As the lions became increasingly aware of their strength, they tested it on everything they could find. For instance, a ground sheet, however large, *had* to be dragged about, and they would set to work in proper feline fashion, placing it under their bodies and pulling it between their front legs, as in later life they would drag a kill. Another favorite game was "king of the castle." A cub would jump onto a potato sack and keep her attacker at bay until she was suddenly dethroned by the other sister coming up from behind. The victor was usually Elsa, who, seeing the other two locked in combat, made the most of her opportunity.

A romp

Our few banana trees were also regarded as delightful toys, and very soon their luxuriant leaves hung in tattered fringes. Tree climbing was another favorite game. The little lions were born acrobats, but often they ventured so high that they could not turn to come down, and we were obliged to rescue them.

When at dawn Nuru let them out, they shot out of doors with a whole night's pent-up energy, and this moment could be compared to the start of a greyhound race. On one such occasion they spotted a tent in which two men who had come to visit us were staying. Within five minutes it was a wreck and we were awakened by the cries of our guests who were vainly trying to rescue their belongings, while the cubs, wild with excitement, dived into the wreckage and reappeared with a variety of trophies—slippers, pajamas, shreds of mosquito netting. We had to enforce discipline that time with a small stick.

Putting them to bed was also no mean task. Imagine three very naughty little girls, who like all children hated bedtime, but who could run twice as fast as those who were in charge of them and had the added advantage of being able to see in the dark.

We were often obliged to resort to subterfuge. One very successful trick was to tie an old bag to a length of rope and drag it steadily toward and then into the pen; usually they could not resist chasing it.

Outdoor games were all very well, but the cubs also developed a fancy for books and cushions. So, to save our library and other possessions, we were eventually obliged to ban them from the house; to effect this we made a shoulder-high door of strong wire on a wooden frame and placed it across the entrance to the veranda. The cubs resented it very much, so to compensate them for their lost playground we hung a tire from a tree, and this proved to be grand for chewing and also as a swing. Another toy we gave them was an empty wooden honey barrel which made a resounding boom when it was pushed. But best of all was a hessian bag. We filled it with old inner tubes and tied it to a branch, from which it dangled invitingly. It had another rope attached to it, and when the cubs hung on to the bag we pulled

The cubs at play (pp. 29-31)

and swung them high up into the air; the more we laughed the better they enjoyed the game.

Yet none of these toys caused them to forget that there was at all times a barrier in front of the veranda, and they often came and rubbed their soft noses against the wire.

Late one afternoon some friends had arrived for a sundowner. Intrigued by the sounds of merriment inside, the cubs soon turned up, but that evening they behaved in a disciplined fashion; there was no nose-rubbing against the wire; all three kept a foot away from it. This exemplary conduct aroused my suspicion, so I got up to investigate its cause. To my horror, I saw a large red spitting cobra between the cubs and the door. In spite of the presence of three lions on one side and of ourselves on the other, it wriggled determinedly across the veranda steps, and by the time we had fetched a shotgun it had disappeared.

No barricades, cobras, or prohibitions made Lustica give up her intention of entering the house; repeatedly she tried all the doors. Pressing a handle proved easy enough; even turning a knob could be done; only when we quickly fitted bolts all around was she defeated, and even so I once caught her trying to push the bolt aside with her teeth. Thwarted in her purpose, she had her revenge upon us, for about this time she tore the laundry off the clothesline and galloped off into the bush with it.

When the cubs were three months old they had teeth big enough to make it possible for them to eat meat. So now I gave them raw minced meat, which was the best we could do to imitate their mother's regurgitated food. For several days they refused to touch it and pulled grimaces of disgust. Then Lustica made the experiment, and found it to her taste. The others took courage from her, and soon there was a fight at every meal. This meant that poor Elsa, who was still weaker than the others, had little chance of getting her fair share, so I kept the titbits for her and used to take her on to my lap for her meals. She loved this; rolling her head from side to side and closing her eyes,

33

Lustica tries the bolt with her teeth

A donkey stalk

she showed how happy she was. At these times she would suck my thumbs and massage my thighs with her front paws as though she were kneading her mother's belly in order to get more milk. It was during these hours that the bond between us developed. We combined playing with feeding, and my days were happily spent with these charming creatures.

They were lazy by nature and it needed a lot of persuasion to get them to move from a comfortable position. Even the most desirable marrow bone was not worth the effort of getting up, and they would roll into position to get at it by the easiest way. But best of all they liked me to hold their bone for them while they lay on their backs, paws in the air, and sucked at it.

When the cubs went into the bush they often had adventures. One morning I was following them, for I had given them a worming powder and wished to see the result. I saw them a little way off asleep. Suddenly I noticed a stream of black soldier ants approaching them. Indeed, some were already climbing up their bodies. Knowing how

34

fiercely these ants will attack anything that lies in their path and how powerful their mandibles are, I was just about to wake up the cubs when the ants changed their direction.

Soon afterwards five donkeys approached and the cubs woke up. This was the first time they had seen such big animals, and they certainly showed the proverbial courage of a lion, for they all charged simultaneously. This put them into such good heart that when, a few days later, our forty pack donkeys and mules came near the house, the three little lions fearlessly put the whole cavalcade to flight.

At five months they were in splendid condition and getting stronger every day. They were quite free except at night, when they slept in an enclosure of rock and sand which led off from their wooden shelter. This was a necessary precaution, for wild lions, hyenas, jackals, and elephants frequently roam around our house, and any of these might have killed them.

The more we grew to know the cubs the more we loved them, so it was hard to accept the fact that we could not keep forever three

35

The cubs at six months

fast-growing lions. Regretfully we decided that two must go and that it would be better that the two big ones, who were always together and less dependent on us than Elsa, should be the ones to leave. Our African servants agreed with our choice; when asked their opinion they unanimously chose the smallest. Perhaps they were influenced by visions of the future and thought: "If there must be a lion in the household, then let it be as small as possible."

As to Elsa, we felt that if she had only ourselves as friends she would be easy to train, not only for life at Isiolo but also as a travelling companion on our safaris.

As a home for Lustica and the Big One, we chose the Rotterdam-Blydorp Zoo and made arrangements for them to make the journey by air.

36

Elsa at six months

Since they would have to leave from the Nairobi airfield, which was one hundred and eighty miles away, we decided to get them accustomed to motoring, and took them for short daily trips in my one-and-a-half-ton truck, which had a wired box body. We also began to feed them in it, so that they might get used to it and consider it as one of their play pens.

On the last day we padded the car with soft sand-bags.

When we drove off, Elsa ran a short way down the drive and then stood with the most mournful expression in her eyes watching the car in which her two sisters were disappearing. I travelled in the back with the cubs and had armed myself with a small first-aid kit fully expecting to be scratched during the long journey. However, my medical precautions were put to shame, for, after an hour of restlessness, the cubs lay on the bags beside me, embracing me with their paws. We travelled like this for eleven hours, delayed by two blow-outs. The lions could not have been more trusting. When we reached Nairobi they looked at me with their large eyes, puzzled to know what to make of all the strange noises and smells. Then the plane carried them off forever from their native land.

After a few days we received a cable announcing the safe arrival of our cubs in Holland. When I visited them, about three years later, they accepted me as a friendly person and allowed me to stroke them, but they did not recognize me. They live in splendid conditions and, on the whole, I was glad to know that almost certainly they had no recollection of a freer life.

39

Where are my sisters?

Elsa Meets Other Wild Animals

W H I L E I was absent in Nairobi, George told me, Elsa was very much upset and never left him for a moment; she followed him around, sat under his office desk, where he was working, and at night slept on his bed. Each evening he took her for a walk, but on the day of my return she refused to accompany him and sat herself down expectantly in the middle of the drive. Nothing would move her. Could it have been that she knew I was coming back? If so, to what animal instinct can one attribute such foreknowledge? Behavior of this kind is difficult if not impossible to explain.

When I arrived alone she gave me a great welcome, but it was heartbreaking to see her searching everywhere for her sisters. For many days to come she gazed into the bush and called for them. She followed us everywhere, evidently fearing that we too might desert her. To reassure her we kept her in the house; she slept on our bed, and we were often wakened by her rough tongue licking our faces.

As soon as we could make the necessary arrangements we took her on safari in order to break this atmosphere of waiting and distress, and luckily she took to all that safari means and loved it as much as we did.

My truck, packed with soft luggage and bedding rolls, was ideal for her to travel in, since, from a comfortable couch, she could watch all that was going on.

We camped by the Uaso Nyiro River, whose banks are lined with doum palms and acacia bush. In the dry season the shallow waters flow slowly down to the Lorian Swamp, passing some rapids and forming many deep pools, which are full of fish.

A Samburu on the move near Isiolo

Near our camp there were rocky ridges. Elsa explored their clefts, sniffed among the rocks, and usually ended by settling herself on the top of some rock from which she could survey the surrounding bush. In the late afternoon the sun turned the country into a blaze of warm colors, and then she blended into the reddish stone as though she were a part of it.

This was the most enjoyable part of the day; everything and everyone relaxed after the great heat; the shadows lengthened and became a deep purple until, by the rapid sinking of the sun, all details were extinguished. A faint bird-call died gradually away, the world grew silent, all was in suspense, awaiting the darkness and, with it, the awakening of the bush. Then the long-drawn call of the hyenas gave the signal and the hunt began.

I remember one particular evening: I secured Elsa to a tree in front of the tents and she started to chew her dinner, while I sat in the darkness and listened.

Pati hopped onto my lap and, nestling comfortably, ground her teeth—a habit which I knew indicated that she was happy. A cicada chirruped near the river, where rippling waters reflected the rising moon. In the soft darkness above, the stars sparkled brilliantly—and in the Northern Frontier they always seem to me to be twice as big as anywhere else. Now I heard a deep vibrating sound like that of distant aircraft; this meant that elephants were making their way to the river. Luckily, the wind was in our favor; and the rumbling soon ceased.

Suddenly, the unmistakable grunts of lion became audible. At first they were very far away, then, gradually, they grew louder and louder. What could Elsa be thinking about all this? In fact, she seemed utterly unconcerned at the approach of her own kind. She tore at her meat, gnawing slices off with her molars, then she rolled on her back, all four paws in the air, and dozed off, while I sat listening to the chuckling of hyena, the yelping of jackal, and the magnificent chorus of the lions.

It is very hot at that season, so Elsa spent part of the day in the water; then, when the sun made this uncomfortable for her, she would

Elephants near Isiolo

rest in the reeds, at intervals rolling lazily into the river, where she landed with a great splash. As we knew that crocodiles were plentiful in the Uaso Nyiro this caused us some concern, but none ever approached her.

Elsa was always full of mischief; sharing her fun with us, she would splash us whenever she found us off guard, or she would jump quickly out of the water, pounce on us, wet as she was, and we would find ourselves rolling in the sand with our cameras, field glasses, and rifles pressed down by her heavy dripping body. She used her paws in a variety of ways. She would use them in gentle caresses, but she could also deliver a playful well-aimed smack at full speed, and she knew a little ju-jitsu trick which unfailingly laid us flat on our backs. No matter how prepared we were for the act, she would give just a small twist to our ankles with her paw and down we went.

Elsa was very particular about her claws; certain trees with a rough bark provided her with the means of sharpening them, and she scratched away, leaving deep lines, until she was satisfied with the result of the operation.[1]

Elsa was not afraid of the sound of a shot, and she grew to know that "bang" meant a dead bird. She loved retrieving, especially guinea fowl, whose quills she crunched, though she very rarely ate the flesh and never the feathers. The first bird was always hers; she would carry it proudly in her mouth till she found this uncomfortable, then she placed it at my feet and looked at me, as though to say: "Please carry it for me," then, so long as I dangled it in front of her nose, she trotted good-naturedly after it.

Strangely enough, though so fond of guinea fowl, she took no interest in francolins, a bird much like an English partridge.

Whenever she discovered some elephant droppings, she at once rolled in them; indeed, it seemed that she regarded them as an ideal bath powder. She hugged the big balls and rubbed the perfume well into her skin. Rhino droppings she also found attractive; in fact, she

[1] In fact she was probably stretching her retractile claw muscles.

44

Elsa learns to retrieve

Elsa retrieves a vulturine guinea fowl

liked the droppings of most herbivorous animals, but preferred those of pachyderms. We often wondered about this behavior—could it come from an instinct to disguise her own scent from the animals that, in a natural state, she would kill and eat? The habit, common to the domestic cat and dog, of rolling in excrement is no doubt a degenerate form of the same instinct. We never saw her roll in the droppings of carnivorous animals.

Elsa was very careful in placing her droppings always a few yards away from the game paths where we usually walked.

One afternoon Elsa rushed off into the bush attracted by the noise of elephant. Soon we heard loud trumpetings and screams and the cackling of guinea fowl as well. In great excitement we awaited the outcome of this meeting. After a while the elephant noises ceased, but to make up for it, the guinea fowl raised a most alarming clatter. Then, to our amazement, Elsa emerged from a thicket closely followed by a flock of vulturine guinea fowl who seemed determined to chase

her away, for whenever she made an attempt to sit down they chuckled and cackled, so that she just had to keep going. Only after these bold birds became aware of our presence was she allowed some peace.

During one of our walks Elsa suddenly froze in front of a cluster of sansevieria bush, then leapt in the air and retreated hastily, giving us a look which seemed to say: "Why don't you do like me?" At this moment we saw a large snake between the pointed sword-sharp sansevieria leaves; it was well protected in the impenetrable thicket of blades, and we thanked Elsa for her warning.

When we returned to Isiolo, the rains had started. The country was covered with little rivulets and pools. This provided fine fun for Elsa; she splashed in every one of them, and, greatly invigorated, proceeded with pouncing leaps to cover us with what she evidently considered to be heavenly mud. This was beyond a joke; we had to make her realize that she had grown too heavy for such light-hearted flying jumps. We explained the situation to her by the judicious use of a small stick; she understood at once, and thereafter we very seldom had to make use of it, though we always carried it as a reminder. By now Elsa also understood the meaning of "No" and she would obey even when tempted by an antelope.

Often, it was touching to see her torn between her hunting instinct and her wish to please us. Anything moving seemed to her, as it would to most dogs, just asking to be chased; but, as yet, her instinct to kill had not fully developed. Of course, we had been careful never to show her her goat meat alive. She had plenty of opportunity of seeing wild animals, but as we were usually with her when this happened, she gave chase merely in play and always came back to us after a short time, rubbed her head against our knees, and told us with a low miaow about the game.

We had animals of all kinds around our house. A herd of water-buck and impala antelope and about sixty reticulated giraffes had been our neighbors for many years. Elsa met them on every walk, and they got to know her very well and even allowed her to stalk them to within a few yards before they quietly turned away, and a family of bat-eared foxes got so used to her that we were able to approach to within a few paces of the burrows of these timid animals while their cubs rolled in the sand in front of the entrance holes, guarded by the parent foxes.

Mongooses also provided Elsa with a lot of fun. These little creatures, no bigger than a weasel, live in abandoned termite hills, which, made as they are of cement-hard soil, constitute ideal fortresses. Standing as high as eight feet and built with many air funnels, they also provide cool shelters during the heat of the day. About teatime the mongoose comedians leave their stronghold and feed on grubs and insects until it becomes dark, when they return home. That was the hour at which our walks often made us pass them. Elsa would sit absolutely still in front of the ant-hill besieging them, apparently deriving great satis-faction from seeing the little clowns popping their heads out of the air funnels, only to give a sharp whistle of alarm and disappear like shadows.

From the start, Elsa dragged a ground sheet as she would later drag a kill

But if the mongooses were fun to tease, the baboons were infuriating. They lived in a leopard-safe dormitory, on a sheer cliff, near our house. There they would spend the night in safety, clinging to the slightest depression in the rock. Before sunset they always retired to this refuge, and the cliff appeared to be covered with black spots. From their safe position they barked and shrieked at Elsa, who could do nothing in retaliation.

It was an exciting moment when the cub met her first elephant, an anxious one too, for poor Elsa had no mother to warn her against these animals who regard lions as the only enemies of their young and there-fore sometimes kill them. One day Nuru, who had taken her out for her morning walk, came back panting to say that Elsa was "playing with an elephant." We took our rifles and he guided us to the scene. There we saw a great old elephant, his head buried in a bush, enjoying his breakfast. Suddenly Elsa, who had crept up from behind, took a playful swipe at one of his hind legs. A scream of shocked surprise and injured dignity followed this piece of impertinence. Then the elephant backed from the bush and charged. Elsa hopped nimbly out of his way and, quite unimpressed, began to stalk him. It was a very funny though an alarming sight, and we could only hope that we should not need to use our guns. Luckily, after a time, both became bored with the game; the old elephant went back to his meal and Elsa lay down, close by, and went to sleep.

During the next few months the cub took every opportunity that came her way to harry elephants, and there were many such occasions for the elephant season was beginning. This meant an annual invasion by herds numbering several hundred animals. The great beasts seemed to be very familiar with the geography of Isiolo and always went to the places where the best maize and brussels sprouts grew. Apart from this and in spite of a dense African population and motor traffic, they behaved very well and gave little trouble. As our home, which is three miles distant from Isiolo, is surrounded by the best browsing, a large number of the invaders come to visit us, and an old rifle range in front of the house has become their favorite playground. At this season, we have therefore to be very careful on our walks for small groups of elephants are always about. Now, having to protect Elsa as well as ourselves made us all the more alert.

One day at noon Nuru and Elsa returned home followed by a large number of elephants; from our dining-room window we could see them in the bush. We tried to divert her attention but she had turned and was determined to meet the advancing herd. Then, suddenly, she sat down and watched them as they turned away and walked in single file across the rifle range. It was a grand parade as one after another emerged from the bush in which Elsa crouched, giving them her scent. She waited until the last of about twenty elephants had crossed, then she followed them slowly, her head held in a straight line with her shoulders, her tail outstretched. Suddenly the big bull in the rear turned and, jerking his massive head at Elsa, screamed with a high-pitched trumpeting sound. This war cry did not intimidate her, and she walked determinedly on; so did the big elephant. We went out and, following cautiously, saw glimpses of Elsa and the elephants mingling together in the undergrowth. There were no screams nor any sound of breaking branches, which would have indicated trouble. All the same, we waited anxiously till eventually the cub reappeared looking rather bored with the whole business.

But not all the elephants which Elsa met were so amiable as these. On another occasion she succeeded in starting a colossal stampede. The first thing we heard was tremendous thundering on the rifle range, and when we reached the scene we saw a herd of elephants racing down-hill, with Elsa close behind them. Finally she was charged by a single bull, but she was much too quick for him and in time he gave up the attack and followed his companions.

Giraffes provided her with great fun too. One afternoon, when we were out with her, she took on fifty. Wriggling her body close to the ground and shivering with excitement, she stalked them, advancing step by step. The giraffes took no notice of her, they just stood and

51

Elsa and the giraffes (pp. 52-53)

watched her nonchalantly. She looked at them and then back at us, as though she wanted to say: "Why do you stand there like candlesticks and spoil my stalking?" Finally she got really cross and, rushing full speed at me, knocked me flat.

Toward sunset, we ran into a herd of elephants. The light was failing rapidly but we could just see the shapes of elephants in all directions.

It has always seemed miraculous to me that these colossal animals can move noiselessly through the bush and are thus able to surround one without warning. This time there was no doubt that we were cut off. Wherever we looked for an opening to slip through an elephant blocked the way. We tried to hold Elsa's attention, for it was not a moment for her to start one of her games with the giants. But all too soon she spotted them and dashed into their midst, then she was beyond our control. We heard screams and shrill piercing cries; my nerves were on edge, for, however carefully we maneuvered through the dark bush, there stood an elephant confronting us. At last we managed to make our way out and reached home, but, of course, without Elsa. She only returned much later; apparently she had had great fun and certainly did not understand why I was a nervous wreck.

A euphorbia hedge borders our drive; no ordinary animal will break through it because it contains a caustic latex. If the smallest drop of this substance touches the eye it burns the membrane most painfully and will inflame it for many days. It is therefore given a wide berth by all animals except elephants, who love eating its juicy twigs and after a night's meal leave big open gaps.

Once, when I was feeding Elsa in her enclosure, I heard the unmistakable rumbling of elephants behind this hedge, which borders her wooden house, and there, sure enough, were five of the giants crunching loudly and making a meal of the only barrier which stood between us. Indeed, at the time I am writing about, the hedge was already a poor sight owing to their attentions.

To add to the excitement of Elsa's life there was now a rhino living close to our house. One evening at dark, when we were returning from a walk, the cub suddenly darted behind the servants' quarters. A tremendous commotion ensued. We went to find out what it was about and saw Elsa and the rhino facing each other. After a few moments of indecision, the rhino, snorting angrily, retreated with the cub in hot pursuit.

The following evening I was walking with Elsa and Nuru—we were late and it was getting dark—when suddenly the Somali grabbed my shoulder, thus preventing me from walking straight into the rhino, which stood behind a bush, facing us. I leapt back and ran. Luckily Elsa, who had not seen the rhino, thought I was playing a game and followed me. This was fortunate, for rhinos are unpredictable creatures who are apt to charge anything, including trucks and trains. The next day, however, Elsa had her fun; she chased the animal for two miles across the valley, Nuru loyally panting behind her. After this experience the rhino took itself off to quieter quarters.

By now we had established a routine for Elsa. The mornings were cool; it was then that we often watched the impala antelope leaping gracefully on the rifle range and listened to the chorus of the awakening birds. As soon as it got light Nuru released Elsa and both walked a short distance into the bush. The cub, full of unspent energy, chased everything she could find, including her own tail.

Then, when the sun got warm, she and Nuru settled under a shady tree and Elsa dozed while he read his Koran and sipped tea. Nuru always carried a rifle to protect them both against wild animals but was very good about following our instructions "to shout before shooting." He was genuinely fond of Elsa and handled her very well.

About teatime the two of them returned and we took over. First, Elsa had some milk, then we wandered into the hills or walked in the plain; she climbed trees, appeared to sharpen her claws, followed exciting scents or stalked Grant's gazelle and gerenuk, which sometimes played hide-and-seek with her. Much to our surprise, she was fascinated by tortoises, which she rolled over and over; she loved play-

55

ing, and never did she miss an opportunity of starting a game with us—we were her "pride" and she shared everything with us.

As darkness fell we returned home and took her to her enclosure, where her evening meal awaited her. It consisted of large quantities of raw meat, mostly sheep and goat; she got her roughage by breaking up the rib bones and the cartilages. As I held her bones for her I would watch the muscles of her forehead moving powerfully. I always had to scratch the marrow out for her; she licked it greedily from my fingers, resting her heavy body upright against my arms. While this went on, Pati sat on the window sill watching us, content to know that soon her turn would come to spend the night cuddled around my neck and that then she would have me to herself.

Till then, I sat with Elsa, playing with her, sketching her, or reading. These evenings were our most intimate time, and I believe that her love for us was mostly fostered in these hours when, fed and happy, she could doze off with my thumb still in her mouth. It was only on moonlight nights that she became restless; then she padded along the wire, listening intently, her nostrils quivering to catch the faintest scent which might bring a message from the mysterious night outside. When she was nervous her paws became damp and I could often judge her state of mind by holding them in my hands.

Elsa Goes to the Indian Ocean

E l s a was now a year old; she had changed her teeth and I had been allowed to wiggle out one milk canine, while she helpfully held her head quite still. To gnaw off her meat she usually used her molars, not her incisors, but her very rough tongue, covered with minute quills, she employed for rasping it from the bone. Her saliva was rich and very salty.

Pati was now getting old, and I kept her as quiet as I could.

Our local leave was due and we planned to spend it by the sea, on a remote part of the coast, close to a small Barjun fishing village and not far from the Somali border. The nearest white population was ninety miles south in Lamu. It would be a perfect place for Elsa, for we could camp on the beach, away from people, with miles of clean sand around us, and a bushy hinterland behind would provide shade.

We took two friends with us, one a young District Officer, Don, and the other, Herbert, an Austrian writer who was our guest.

It was a long journey over bad tracks and it took us three days. I usually went ahead with Elsa in my truck, George and the others following in two Land Rovers with Pati. The country through which we passed was dry, sandy, and hot.

One day the road became a network of camel spoor. When it was getting dark I lost my way, ran out of petrol, and, hoping that George would follow my tracks, waited for him. Only after several hours did I see his lights. When he arrived he said that our camp was already pitched some miles away and told me we must hurry back as he had left Pati very ill with heat stroke.

He had given her some brandy to strengthen her but had little hope. The miles back to the camp seemed endless to me. I found Pati in a coma. Her heart was beating so rapidly that it was improbable that it would stand the strain much longer. Gradually she became semiconscious, recognized me, and made a weak attempt to grind her teeth. This had always been her way of showing her affection; it was her last message to me. Later she grew calm and her heart slowed down till it had almost ceased to beat; then suddenly her little body quivered in a last convulsion, stretched stiffly, and collapsed.

Pati was dead.

I held her close. Her warm body took a long time to cool.

I thought of the many moments of happiness she had given me in the seven and a half years during which we had shared our lives. On how many safaris had she been my companion. She had been with me to Lake Rudolf, where the heat had been a great strain on her; to the coast, where she had spent many hours cramped in a dhow; to Mount Kenya, whose moorlands she had loved; to the Suguta valley and Mount Nyiro, where she had cleverly hung on to the mule which I rode across precipitous tracks; she had been with me to camping places all over Kenya, when I was painting the African tribes. Sometimes for months on end she had been my only friend.

How tolerant she was of the bush babies, squirrels, and mongooses which came and went in our household, and how she loved the lions. At meals she sat by my plate and took the titbits gently from my hand.

She had become part of me.

Now I wrapped her in a cloth, fastened her harness and leash round it, and carried her some distance away from the camp. Here I dug her grave. The night was hot and the moonlight softened the shadows in the wide plain around us. All was still and so peaceful.

The next morning we drove on and I was glad that the bad road held my attention.

It was late afternoon when we reached the coast and fishermen who came out to greet us told us that a lion was causing a great deal of trouble. Almost nightly it raided their goats and they very much hoped that George would kill it.

There was no time to make a proper camp, so we put our beds out in the open. I was the only woman among four Europeans and six Africans, and I placed mine at a little distance away. Elsa was secured in my truck next to me. Soon everyone went to sleep except myself. Suddenly I heard a dragging noise and flashed my torch; there, a few yards from my bed, was a lion with the skin of the buck we had shot that afternoon in its mouth.

For a second I wondered if it might be Elsa, but then I saw her in the back of my car. I looked again; the lion was still staring at me, and now he was growling.

I moved slowly toward George and, stupidly, turned my back on the lion. We were only a few paces from each other and I felt that he was following me, so I turned and shone my torch into his face; by then we were about eight yards apart. I walked backward toward the camp beds where the men were snoring. Only George woke up. When I told him that a lion was following me he said: "Nonsense, probably a hyena or a leopard." All the same he picked up his heavy rifle and went in the direction I indicated, and there, sure enough, he soon saw two eyes and heard the growl of a lion. He had little doubt that this was the troublesome lion we had been told about; so he tied a large piece of meat to a tree some thirty yards in front of the car and decided to sit up and wait for him.

After a short time we heard a clatter coming from behind the cars where our evening meal had been cooked.

George crept around, levelled his rifle, and flashed his torch there; he saw the lion sitting among the pots and pans finishing off the remains of our dinner. He pressed the trigger, only a click sounded; he pressed it again, with the same result. He had forgotten to load the rifle! The lion got up and sauntered off. Sheepishly George loaded the rifle and went back to his post.

Much later he heard something tugging at the meat and switched on

Surprisingly, Elsa loved the sea

the car lights; then he saw the lion brilliantly illuminated and shot him through the heart.

He was a young maneless lion, typical of the coast region.

When light broke we investigated his pugmarks and discovered that he had first seized the skin of the antelope, then dragged it to within twenty yards of my bed, where he had eaten his meal. When replete he had made a leisurely round of the camp. Of all these goings-on Elsa had been an interested spectator, but she had never uttered a sound.

As soon as the sun was up the whole camp trooped down to the water's edge to introduce her to the Indian Ocean. The tide was receding; at first she was nervous of the unaccustomed roar and rush of the waves. Then she sniffed cautiously at the water, bit at the foam; finally she put her head down to drink, but her first mouthful of salt water made her wrinkle her nose and pull grimaces of disgust. How-

ever, when she saw the rest of the party enjoying a bath, she decided
to trust us and join in the fun. Very soon she became quite water-
crazy. Rain pools and shallow rivers had always excited and invigorated
her, but this great ocean was a real heaven for her. She swam effort-
lessly, far out of her depth; ducked us and splashed the water with her
tail and ensured that we too swallowed mouthfuls of salt water before
we were able to escape from her antics.

She followed us everywhere, so I usually stayed behind when the
others went fishing; otherwise she would have swum out after our
boat.

The reef in this place was the best of all those along the Kenya
coast for coral fish. Armed with harpoons and goggles, we dived into
a fascinating world. Some of the corals were pagoda-shaped, others
looked like the brains of giants, while some fanned out like mushrooms

61

patterned with purple rosettes or furrowed by emerald creases. Curtains of brilliant-colored seaweed, in the folds of which schools of minute fish were hiding, fingered the current. We swam through deep valleys, which often led into caverns, and we peeped into dimly lit tunnels, out of whose depths coral fish emerged, inquisitive and puzzled by our monstrous bulk; they had good reason for their surprise, since under water everything looks twice its natural size.

We saw fish resembling red striped porcupine when swimming, which changed their quills to feathery wings while hovering like butterflies close to a coral. Some, like golden boxes dotted with spots of blue, had cowlike horns above their eyes; some were of deepest blue, recalling seas, with yellow maps of Africa drawn upon their flattened sides; some looked like colored chess-boards, some like zebras; some had masks and trailed their elongated fins like floating veils between them. Some puffers bloated their balloons and threw up quills like hedgehogs in defense; some thrust up an inch-long knife behind the dorsal fin, in fear; some lay out flat upon the floor, like giant sole, well camouflaged among the shifting sand. There were the buried clams, their mouths a deadly trap, just showing above ground; the deadly poisonous stone fish, whose puff adder markings were concealed by bright red fringes and which kept so still against a coral rock, except for amber-colored eyes, which followed every move and gave the fish away. Then there were crayfish with their sharp hooked armor; however threatening they looked they were far the easiest to shoot. They waited stupidly, half hidden under rocks, for the harpoon to penetrate their shell, between the eyes. Their long thin antennae floated at alert, but rarely warned in time to let the fish escape. The sea anemones, which seemed to us a mass of lovely flowers, were fatal to small organisms, which swam between their ever-moving tentacles. Luckily, the poison rays were always quicker than we and shot off long before we could detect their blue-spotted shapes, hidden in the sand.

While we glided fascinated through this world of luminous iridescent colors and fairy shapes, Elsa, with someone to keep her company, rested in the shade of a mangrove tree close to the camp. When passing fishermen got to know of this they made a big detour, hitched up their loincloths, and waded into the sea. They would have felt less reassured had they known what an amphibious creature she was.

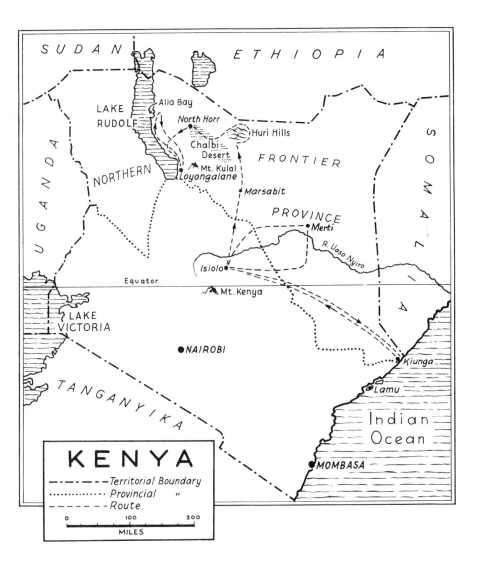

SUDAN

ETHIOPIA

UGANDA

NORTHERN

LAKE
RUDOLF

Alia Bay

North Horr

Chalbi
Desert

Huri Hills

FRONTIER

Mt. Kulal
Loyongalane

Marsabit

PROVINCE

Merti

R. Uaso Nyiro

SOMALIA

Isiolo

Equator

Mt. Kenya

LAKE
VICTORIA

NAIROBI

Kiunga

Lamu

TANGANYIKA

Indian
Ocean

MOMBASA

KENYA

—·—·—·—Territorial Boundary
················· Provincial "
— — — — —Route

0   100   200
MILES

She loved walking along the beach, where she chased the coconuts bobbing in the surf, getting splashed and swamped by the waves in the process. Sometimes we tied a string to a coconut and swung it in a circle above our heads while she jumped high up after it as it flew past. She soon discovered that digging in the sand was a most rewarding game, since the deeper the hole the wetter and cooler it became and therefore the nicer to roll in. Often she dragged long strands of seaweed along, entangling herself in it till she looked like some odd sea monster. But crabs provided her with the best fun of all. Toward sunset the beach became alive with these little pink creatures shuffling sideways in order to get from their holes to the water, only to be washed ashore again a moment later. Persistently they shuffled, only to be thrown back again, until finally their patience was rewarded and they grabbed some piece of delicious seaweed and pulled it into their hole before the next wave was able to carry it off. Elsa did not make things easier for the busy creatures; she would rush from one to the other, invariably getting nipped in the nose, but undeterred she pounced again, only to be nipped once more. To the crabs' credit be it recorded that of all Elsa's opponents they were the only ones, not excluding elephants, buffaloes, and rhinos, which stood their ground. Sideways on they waited in front of their holes, one pink claw erect, and, however cunningly Elsa tried to outwit them, they were always quicker than she was and her soft nose got punctured again.

Feeding Elsa became quite a problem, for the local fishermen were quick to recognize the source of income which she represented, and the price of goats soared. In fact, for some time she kept the villagers in luxuries hitherto unknown to them. However, in the end, she had her revenge. The herdsmen never guarded their animals, which straggled along all day in the bush, an easy prey to leopards and lions. One evening we were out on the beach, long after bedtime for goats, when Elsa suddenly darted into a bush; there followed a loud bleat and then silence. She must have scented a lone straggler, pounced on the goat, and squashed it with her weight. But, never having killed before, she

64

did not know what to do next, and when we arrived she plainly asked us for help. While Elsa held the animal down George quickly shot the beast. As no complaint was made by the owner for its loss, which was no doubt credited to the usual kill of some wild lion, we kept quiet about the incident. Had we done otherwise every moribund goat from a day's march north and south of the camp would have been left out for Elsa to devour so that compensation might be claimed. We overcame our qualms of conscience with the thought that George had rid the district of its chief goat-eater and also with the recollection of the exorbitant prices we had paid for the most miserable little beasts which we had bought on Elsa's behalf.

Toward the end of our holiday George became ill with malaria. But he was so keen on fishing that he took much stronger doses of mepacrine than the normal one and also got up before he should, to go goggling.

Returning home one evening from a walk along the beach with Elsa, as I neared the camp I heard an alarming howling and screaming. After securing Elsa in my truck, I rushed to the tent, where I found George limp and collapsed in a chair. He was emitting frightful groans and yelling for his revolver, for me, cursing Elsa, and shouting that he wanted to shoot himself. Even in his semiconscious condition he recognized me, seized me with an iron grip, and said that now that I was there he could relax and die. I was most alarmed; the boys stayed a few yards away looking very frightened. Our friend stood helpless, clutching a stick with which he proposed to club George if he should become violent.

In whispers, they told me that quite suddenly George had started to gesticulate wildly, shrieking for me and shouting for his revolver to kill himself. Luckily, I had returned soon after he had collapsed. The main thing now was to carry him to his bed and try to calm him. He hung lifeless and icy cold in our arms as we moved him. Although my heart was heavy with fear, I began talking to him in a quiet voice, telling him about our walk along the beach, about the fish we were going to eat for dinner, about a shell I had found, and made fun of his strange behavior. But all the time I wondered whether he were not going to die. Like a child, he responded to my efforts to soothe him and calmed down. But his temples grew gray, his nostrils fell in, and his eyes closed. He whispered that an icy current was creeping up his legs toward his heart, that his arms were equally lifeless and cold, and that when both ice waves met at his heart he would die. Suddenly he was seized by panic, clutched me with a desperate strength, as though hanging on to life. I poured brandy between his dry lips, stroked him gently, and, trying to divert his mind toward some action associated with the near future, told him about his birthday cake which I had brought all the way from Isiolo, and said that we should eat it that night, as soon as he was well enough to get up.

I knew the cause of his condition: he had been poisoned by an overdose of mepacrine; the violence of the reaction was due to the fact that he had gone goggling without giving this dangerous drug time to work. He had had a similar experience many years ago, and from this I recognized the symptoms. Before he fell into an exhausted sleep, the night had passed; during that time he had had several relapses, during which his brain worked with frightening rapidity while he uttered senseless words. The next morning I sent to Lamu for a doctor, but the competent Indian who came could do little for George except to order sleeping drugs and give him confidence that he was going to recover provided he did not go goggling again.

As soon as George was well enough, we returned to Isiolo. Like all holidays, ours had passed much too quickly, but by the time we went home we had acquired a deep tan and Elsa, owing to her sea bathing, had developed a beautiful silky coat.

The Man-Eating Lions

O N E day, soon after our return to Isiolo, I noticed that Elsa walked with difficulty, and was in pain. It was getting dark and a long distance of steep rocky slopes, covered with thornbush, lay between us and home. Soon Elsa could walk no farther. George thought that she might be suffering from constipation and suggested that I should give her an enema on the spot. That meant returning home and then driving to Isiolo to get what was needed. While I did this, he remained with Elsa.

By the time everything was ready it was dark, then I had to struggle up the hills, carrying warm water, an enema, and a lamp. It is one thing to administer an enema in a vet's surgery, but it is quite another to do this among thorn-covered bush and in the dark to a wildly scratching lion.

I congratulated myself when I had inserted a pint of liquid into poor Elsa, but that was all she would tolerate and it was, of course, far too little to produce any results, so we had no choice left but to carry her home.

Again, I stumbled back to the house, where I collected a camp bed, to use as a stretcher, a few torches, and six boys to act as porters. The procession then moved up the hill.

When we arrived Elsa rolled at once onto the bed, where, lying on her back, she showed that she was thoroughly enjoying this queer mode of transport. Indeed it seemed as though she had never travelled in any other way. But as she weighed at least a hundred and eighty pounds, her pleasure was not shared by the porters as they sweated and panted, struggling downhill, stopping every few minutes to rest.

Elsa made no attempt to leave the stretcher, but she had great fun giving an occasional nip on the bottom to the nearest boy, as if to urge him on.

When at last we reached home—all of us, except Elsa, quite exhausted—we were obliged to roll her off the bed, for she had no intention of leaving it voluntarily.

Later we discovered that hookworm was the cause of her trouble. She must have got infected with it when we were on the coast.

It was not long after she had recovered that George had to deal with two man-eating lions which, during the past three years, had killed or mauled about twenty-eight people of the Boran tribe. Many and gruesome were the tales told of their marauding. On a dark evening one of the lions had forced his way into a *boma*[1] and seized a youth, who called loudly for help as he was being dragged away. No one had dared move. Only two dogs went to his rescue; they ran after him barking, thus causing the lion to drop his prey and chase them instead, but having done this the lion had returned to his victim, whose cries gradually faded into the distance.

As a rule the Boran are very brave indeed, and are among the few African tribes who still hunt lions with a spear.[2]

They also kill elephants not for food but for spear blooding, or to prove their manhood. When elephants are located there is great excitement and fierce competition among the young men. Each tries to be the first to blood his spear; the one who does, claims the trophy. No

---

[1] The word *boma* originally meant a defended place. It is now used to describe an administrative post, as well as any enclosed African habitation.

[2] Two other ancient forms of hunting still survive—the whalers who go out in little boats with primitive harpoons and the Pygmies (who kill, mainly for food); when they go out after elephants, one man crawls under the animal's belly and stabs him, then he goes back to his companions, and only after that do the others join in the hunt.

Elsa goes hunting with George

young man is looked upon with favor by the girls until he has won his spurs by killing some dangerous animal.

But brave as the Boran are, in this case the man-eaters completely overawed them. This was partly due to the cunning and boldness of the lions, partly to the fact that, when hunted, they would always retreat into dense riverine undergrowth, where it was impossible for a man to poise and throw a spear. Superstition had also added its quota to the fear with which they were regarded. It was said that before starting off on a raid the lions would repair to an open sandy place and there make two rows of depressions in the sand with their paws. Then, using twigs as counters, they would play the ancient game of *bau* (a game of unknown antiquity, which resembles draughts and is played all over Africa). If the omens were good they would raid a *boma* and claim a victim; if not, they would wait. Another story had it that the lions were the spirits of two "holy men" who had been murdered, long ago, by the Boran and who had now come back in this shape to seek their revenge. So strongly was this view held that the

local Boran had petitioned a practicing "holy man" to come from a great distance to exorcise the spirits. He came with book, bell, and candle and charged a fee of sixty goats, but the lions continued their depredations. To add to the legend of the lions' invulnerability, George and other hunters had tried on previous occasions to kill them and had failed, owing to lack of time. This confirmed the Boran's opinion that the lions were supernatural beings and that it was useless to hunt them.

So now, in spite of the coming rains, we were determined to break the spell. Little did we realize that it would take us twenty-four days and nights to accomplish our task. We set off, Elsa and myself in the truck; George, a young officer on leave from the King's African Rifles, and a few Game Scouts in the Land Rover and a trailer. We were fortunate to find a good camping site a couple of miles short of Merti trading center. Here we placed our tents under some fine acacia trees, near the edge of the riverine bush and about half a mile from the Uaso Nyiro River. It was set well in the open, an important point when dealing with man-eaters, for they are less likely to raid a camp placed in the open than one surrounded by bush.

After pitching camp, we went into Merti to get the latest news of the man-eaters. The place consisted of three mud and corrugated-iron shops owned by Somalis. They told us that for the last three months the lions had not killed a human being but that they had persistently raided livestock. Only a few nights before they had broken into the yard at the back of the principal shop and taken a donkey, and almost every night for the past four weeks they had been heard roaring up and down the river.

George sent at once for the local headman and elders of the Boran and ordered them to inform their people living along the river that as soon as the lions killed again news was to be brought to him.

These lions covered an area of fifty miles along the Uaso Nyiro River. From the beginning it seemed as if they were aware of our intentions. They had the terrain in their favor and made good use of the almost impenetrable river undergrowth. They were most energetic walkers and thought nothing of covering thirty miles during a night, but they at least did this in the cool, while we were obliged to follow in the heat of the day, plodding through thick bush, with sharp thorns and palm fronds obscuring our view, or wading knee-deep in swamp and slush through marshy lagoons.

To begin with, George had to cover forty miles before he was able to shoot a zebra; he then towed its carcass into the riverine undergrowth about a mile from our camp and secured it on the ground under an acacia tree, in the lower branches of which, about twelve feet from the ground, we built a machan, or platform. For the next three nights George and John, the young officer, kept watch. We heard the lions roaring upriver but nothing happened. I sat in camp listening to their magnificent chorus, with Elsa snoring contentedly by my side, inside the truck. Did she not know that her own kin were near by? The paradox of the situation came clearly to my mind: here we were hunting dangerous man-eaters by day and by night, yet when we returned exhausted and defeated we looked forward to being with Elsa, who compensated us for the fatigue and strain by her affection. Lion versus lion? Whatever the relationship, I could not help admiring these wild creatures, and George, even though he had every reason to bear them a grudge, since he had once been severely mauled by a lion, regarded them as the most intelligent of all wild animals and held them in respect.

On the fourth night, weary from sitting up, he and John slept in camp; it was that night that the lions came to the remains of the kill. Now another carcass had to be obtained, and once more they sat over it for three nights without result. Then once again, exhausted by days spent trying to follow the lions' spoor and sleepless nights, they returned to camp. Once more the lions took the occasion and came to the kill. By that time we were all half inclined to agree with the Boran that perhaps the lions were the spirits of holy men or more likely of devils.

Now we changed our tactics and did most of our hunting by day, following the spoor into dense bush. Twice we got close to the lions only to hear them break away ahead without giving us the chance of a shot. Hunting on foot was most exhausting, not only on account of the heat, but because we had constantly to walk in a crouching position through tunnels in the dense vegetation; nor did the presence of rhinos and elephants make our task easier. The rains had started up-country, and the river already showed signs of rising. As the lions kept to the other side of it, we had to move camp without delay if we were to get across the ford below Merti.

We packed up camp and arrived early in the morning at the ford to find that the water had risen considerably during the night and was still going up; we decided that it was still just fordable by cars, though a little stick which I had stuck into the ground to mark the water level was soon submerged and then swept away. George unhitched the trailer from the Land Rover and removed the fan belt to prevent water from splashing over the ignition system, then it crept into the river and crossed successfully. Next my truck entered with Elsa, as usual, sitting in the back. The water rushed past at alarming speed, carrying debris. The truck got bravely into the middle, then the engine spluttered and died. Nothing would make it start again. We released Elsa at once; she plunged into the water, splashed about, and tried to retrieve the driftwood, as though we had arranged all this for her amusement. Indeed, she had such fun ducking the men who were wading shoulder-high carrying the loads across that we were finally obliged to tie her up. When at last the truck was empty, we tried to tow it, but it leaned alarmingly to one side and the chains we had brought with us were not long enough, so we had rapidly to improvise extensions with buffalo hide. Eventually, all hands pushing and pulling, and applauded by the ever present baboons, we managed to get it across.

Camp had to be pitched on the spot, as it took all the rest of the day to dry out our kit, medicines, ammunition, books, foods, the engine of the truck, car spares, bedding rolls, and tents. Elsa spent her time sniffing the still life, including George's tobacco, which made her grimace in disgust.

By the next morning the river overflowed its banks and we had to move to high ground. During the next night it had rained solidly, and we feared this might mean the end of the lion hunt. Nevertheless we spent the morning looking for a suitable tree in which to conceal a machan, but the bush here was low and we had eventually to content ourselves with a Mswaki-bush, which was hardly high enough to hold a machan above the reach of hungry lions. George shot a zebra and put its carcass beneath the bush for the lions, then, soon after dark, he and John took up watch. Perhaps the lions knew how inadequate the machan was, only eight feet from the ground, for after about an hour the men heard two of them. One was roaring by the ford half a mile away, the other across the river. The roars from the direction of the ford gradually grew louder, and there was no doubt that that lion was in fine voice, for the last roar fairly shook the machan. Next, George heard the unmistakable sound of the lion tearing at the carcass, but it was a dark night and he could not see anything. They waited for the lion to settle down to his meal, then John switched on his torch and the animal became visible; he had his tail toward them and, with his head buried in the carcass, offered a poor shot, till, disturbed by the light, he turned his head and looked toward the machan.

George then aimed at his neck and fired. There was a deep grunt, and the lion leapt into the air and made off, uttering loud gurgling sounds. Evidently he had been hard hit, and George was confident of finding him dead at dawn. As soon as it was light enough two Game Scouts came to the machan from the camp and with George and John followed the blood spoor, which led into the dense bush bordering the river.

If the lion were still alive it was a very dangerous proposition to follow him up. They advanced cautiously step by step, pausing every few minutes, with ears strained to catch the slightest sound. Suddenly there was a growl and George caught a fleeting glimpse of two lions making off; evidently the one from across the river had come to meet his friend. They thought that the next time they neared them the wounded lion would be certain to charge. By now the blood trail had almost disappeared and it was difficult to follow the pugmarks in the uncertain light. They had stopped and were carefully examining the

The engine died in midstream

ground when a Game Scout tapped George on the shoulder and pointed back. There, fifteen yards away, he saw the head of a lion looking at them over a low bush. He shot him between the eyes: a big lion, nine feet five inches from the tip of the nose to the end of his tail. George was sure that it must be the animal he had wounded as there appeared to be two bullet holes in the back of his head, besides the one between the eyes. He assumed that the other lion had escaped across the river and indeed thought he remembered hearing a splash after he had fired.

When I arrived on the battlefield, I gave George full marks for his success. It must have been very frightening to follow a wounded man-eating lion into that thicket. Although we had just spent three weeks hunting these man-eaters, straining every nerve to catch a sight of their golden skins through the underbrush, this was the first time that I had actually seen one of them. Now, his strength was broken; his paws, whose great pugmarks we knew so well, lay limp. He was in the prime of life, about eight years old. Of course we were relieved that at last one of the man-eaters was dead, but, illogically, we did not enjoy our victory over this splendid animal. After the skinning, I photographed its heart; it was as big as a child's head; then I understood why I often felt Elsa's heart throbbing like a motor against her ribs.

George's improvised boat

That night George and John sat up over the zebra hoping that the second man-eater would come; they only got drenched for their pains, but heard a lion roar across the river.

Since the water was now too deep to ford and too dangerous, on account of crocodiles, to swim, George made a boat using the steel frame of a camp bed covered with a ground sheet. It was a great success but unfortunately it could only carry one person. So he crossed alone in it and walked to Merti, where the news of the death of one of the man-eaters aroused much amazement and excitement; now, at last, the Boran were convinced that the lions were less than immortals and were keen to help to find the other one. On the way to Merti George had crossed the fresh spoor of a lioness; this made him wonder whether it was not her voice that he had heard on the previous night. So he began to question whether the lion he had killed was in fact the one which he had previously wounded; it was not impossible that the expanding bullet from his heavy rifle had smashed the beast's skull and so perhaps the two holes at the back of the head were made by fragments of the same bullet. In that case, there was still a wounded lion on the side of the river on which our camp was pitched.

When George crossed back to our side of the river he found a party of six young Boran at the ford, all armed with spears and ready to help look for this possibly wounded lion. He suggested that they should return next day with their best hunting dogs. In the morning we met them, as arranged, and found them accompanied by the most unlikely-looking hunting dogs, which, however, they assured us were not afraid of lions.

Once more we entered the bush; after a short time George noticed that the dogs were not displaying much eagerness to go forward in spite of encouragement from their masters. Then the pack leader turned with his tail between his legs and headed for home with the rest following him. We all expected to hear a roar followed by a charging lion, but nothing happened. Instead, we heard the excited barking of baboons, a sure sign that they had seen something alarming,

either a lion or a leopard; after pausing, with ears and eyes strained, we moved on. Then, as George stooped to pass under a bush, something light-colored caught his eye; in a real fortress of thornbush crouched a lion, apparently ready to charge. George was about to fire when the loud buzzing of flies told him that the animal was dead. We found that the bullet fired from the machan had torn its throat, probably damaging the jugular vein. It was a really magnificent lion, nine feet from tip to tip, not as large as the other, but a much handsomer animal, and I felt like saluting the great beast though he had caused so much terror.

Both lions were in perfect condition, about middle-aged, as lions go. Certainly they had no disabilities to justify their man-eating.

Most lions take to man-eating because they have some infirmity: either they have been wounded by an arrowhead or damaged in a trap, or their teeth are in bad condition, or they have porcupine quills in their paws, or they are very old and in this state turn to less agile forms of food than is natural to them. But there are exceptions, cases where one can only guess at the whim of nature which has induced them to hunt human flesh. Has this taste been aroused by the carelessness of the tribesmen who often sleep at night outside the thorn fence which protects their livestock? If a hungry lion who was considering the painful act of breaking through the fence to kill an animal inside were to find a dinner asleep outside, he would be tempted indeed; could he be blamed for taking the easier course? Such a happening might well become a habit and give birth to another man-eater. Naturally his cubs would learn his way of hunting, and so the trait might be carried on by teaching rather than by hereditary instinct.

Now our task was accomplished, and the Boran would no more be troubled by the spirits of the "holy men." We reflected, however, that there was good reason to suppose that the two lions had sired several lusty cubs and we could only hope that they had not been trained to their fathers' tastes.[1]

[1] Unfortunately, we had evidence recently that this was the case.

79

Elsa is restrained from going after baboons

Safari to Lake Rudolf

E L S A was now eighteen months old and I noticed, for the first time, that she had, temporarily as it proved, developed a strong smell. She had two glands, known as the anal glands, under the root of her tail; these exuded a strong-smelling secretion which she ejected with her urine against certain trees, and although it was her own smell she always pulled up her nose in disgust at it.

One afternoon, after we had returned to Isiolo, we met a herd of eland. Elsa instantly began to stalk them. These large antelope were grazing on a steep slope and had several young among them. One eland cow waited for her and before she got too close to the calves distracted her attention from the youngsters by playing hide-and-seek with her in the bushes. In this way, she kept her engaged until the herd and the calves had safely disappeared beyond the hillside. Then the eland cow galloped off at high speed, leaving poor Elsa standing.

Another case of animal diplomacy was fascinating to watch. We had taken Elsa up a hill behind the house, from the top of which we saw a herd of about eighty elephants, with many small calves feeding below. Elsa saw them too and before we could shout "No" she went off downhill and, a few moments later, was advancing cautiously toward the herd.

Nearest to her was a cow with a small calf. Elsa stalked it with great cunning, but the mother elephant was well aware of her intention. We watched, tense with anxiety, expecting a charge, but to our surprise the mother elephant moved quietly between Elsa and the calf, pushing it slowly toward some big bulls, keeping our lioness on the far side. Disappointed, Elsa looked for the next best playmate and used careful cover to join two feeding bulls. But again she was ignored. Then she tried to provoke other small groups of elephants, advancing to within a few yards of them. Still nothing happened. The sun was getting low; we shouted to her but she obstinately disregarded our calls. Finally we had no alternative but to return home without her. She certainly intended to take her time and we could only rely on her intelligence to keep her out of trouble.

I waited for her inside the enclosure, reading, but my thoughts were not on the book. Horrible visions played tricks with my imagination and I became more and more worried. What could we do? Chaining Elsa up during the elephant season would only frustrate and infuriate her; indeed, it might end by making her dangerous. We had to let her learn her limitations by experience, allow her to weigh the boredom against the fun, or danger, of playing with these big animals. In doing so perhaps she would come to lose interest in them. By this time she was three hours overdue and I feared an accident, then suddenly I heard her familiar hnk-hnk and in she came, very thirsty indeed, yet before she went to her water bowl she licked my face and sucked my thumbs as if to tell me how glad she was to be with me again. She smelled strongly of elephant, and I could well imagine how close she had been to them, and that she had rolled in their droppings. By the way she flung herself with a crash to the ground I could also judge how tired she was. I felt very humble; here was my friend just returned from a world that was utterly denied to me, yet she was as affectionate as ever. Did she have any realization of the extraordinary link she was between the two worlds?

Of all animals, giraffes were undoubtedly her favorites. Often she stalked them until both sides became tired. Then she would sit down waiting for the giraffes to return, and sure enough, after a time they would approach again, advancing slowly step by step, facing Elsa, looking at her with their large sad eyes, while their slender necks arched in an inquisitive way. Then usually, browsing at their favorite acacia seeds as they went by, they would walk peacefully away. But sometimes Elsa would drive them in proper lion fashion. After spotting them, she would turn off at right angles downwind, crouching with her belly close to the ground, every muscle quivering, until she had encircled the herd, then she would drive it toward us. No doubt we were expected to wait in ambush and kill the victims she had so cleverly rounded up for us.

Other animals also attracted her attention; for instance, one day she sniffed the air and then dashed into a thick bush. Soon afterwards we heard crashing and snorting coming straight at us! Quickly we jumped out of the way as a wart hog thundered past, with Elsa hot on his heels. Both disappeared at lightning speed, and for a long time we heard them breaking through the wood. We were very worried for Elsa's safety, as the wart hog has formidable tusks which he can use to kill, till she returned; the winner of the chase rubbed her head against our knees and told us about her new playmate.

Our next safari was to take us to Lake Rudolf, a stretch of brackish water, some one hundred and eighty miles long, reaching to the Ethiopian frontier. We were to be away for seven weeks and most of the time we should travel on foot with pack donkeys and mules. It would be Elsa's first experience of a foot safari in the company of donkeys, and we could only hope that both sides would accept each other. We were quite a party: George and myself, Julian, a Game Warden from a neighboring territory, Herbert, who was again our guest, as well as Game Scouts, drivers, and personal servants, six sheep to feed Elsa on the way, and thirty-five donkeys and mules. The pack animals were sent off three weeks ahead to meet us on the shores of the lake, while we travelled the distance of about three hundred miles by motor transport.

It was a big convoy: two Land Rovers, my one-and-a-half ton truck with Elsa in the back of it, and two three-ton trucks. The latter were necessary to enable us to carry, as well as the men, sufficient food and petrol for the weeks we should be away, also eighty gallons of water.

Our first one hundred and eighty miles led us through the sandy, hot, and dusty plains of the Kaisut desert. Then we ascended the volcanic slopes of the Marsabit mountain, an isolated volcanic mass rising to forty-five hundred feet out of the surrounding desert. Clothed in thick, cool, lichen-covered forest, and often enveloped in mist, it presented a welcome contrast to the hot arid country below. It is a game paradise and harbors elephants carrying some of the finest ivory in Africa, besides rhinos, buffaloes, the greater kudu, lions, and lesser game. Here was the last Administrative Post.

From now on we made our way through practically uninhabited country and were cut off from any contact with the outside world. Nothing broke the monotony of the sand gullies and lava ridges. The only incident was a crash which nearly broke my car in half. One back wheel left us and we came to an abrupt stop. Poor Elsa; it took hours to repair the damage and she had to spend the time inside the car, since it provided the only shade from the fierce sun, which she hated. However, she was most co-operative and, although she did not like strange Africans, obligingly put up with the jabbering crowd of our people, who pressed close to the car trying to be helpful. When we were mobile again, we climbed up the most shocking track into the Huri hills on the Ethiopian border. These are desolate and, though higher than Marsabit, attract less moisture. An enervating gale blows across their slopes and, in consequence, they are barren of forest. Elsa was quite bewildered by the fierce wind and had to spend the night in the truck, well protected with canvas curtains from its icy blast.

George's purpose in visiting these hills was to examine the game situation and to see whether there were any signs of poaching by the Gabbra tribesmen. After a few days spent in patrolling the country we turned westward, crossing the most depressing, desolate lava country, where sharp rocks jerked the car mercilessly, and Elsa had a tough time as we pushed the vehicles through deep sandy river beds or ground our way carefully between boulders, jostling against the large stones. At last we came out on to the Chalbi desert, a dry ancient lake bed some eighty miles in length, with a smooth fairly firm surface on which a vehicle can travel at full speed. Mirages are the most remarkable feature of this area: great expanses of water with palm trees reflected in their surface appear but swiftly vanish as one approaches them. Here, too, gazelles assume the proportions of elephants and appear to be walking on the waters. It is a land of thirst and grilling heat. At the western end of Chalbi lies the oasis of North Horr, where there is a Police Post, and where thousands of camels, sheep, and goats belonging to the Rendille tribe come to water. Another remarkable sight to be seen there in the morning is that of thousands of sand grouse flying in to drink at the few pools. Now soon, as there was nothing to keep us at North Horr, we filled our water containers and continued on our way.

At last, after two hundred and thirty miles of hustling and bumping, we reached Loyongalane, an oasis of fresh-water springs in a grove of doum palms near the south of Lake Rudolf. Here we found our donkeys waiting for us. We took Elsa at once to the lake, which was two miles distant. She rushed into the water as though to throw off the strain of the journey and plunged in right among the crocodiles, which are very plentiful in Lake Rudolf. Luckily, they were not aggressive, but all the same we tried to scare them away. During our safari, their floating, horny shapes, silhouetted all along the shore, were to make bathing, at least for us, a dubious pleasure.

At Loyongalane we established our base camp and spent the next three days in repairing saddlery and packing donkey loads. Each load weighed approximately fifty pounds, two to each donkey. At last all was ready. There were eighteen donkeys loaded with food and camping gear, four with water containers, one riding mule for anyone who went weak or lame, and five spare donkeys. I was worried about what Elsa's attitude toward the donkeys was going to be. She watched all our repacking with restrained interest, then when we started loading she had to be chained up, for the sight of so much lovely meat braying and kicking and rolling in the sand in an endeavor to throw

Elsa strides into Lake Rudolf

off unwanted burdens, with shouting Africans rushing about trying to bring order into the chaos, made her tense with excitement. The main cavalcade started off in the morning and we followed with Elsa later in the day when it was cooler. Our march was northward along the shore line. Elsa was very excited and rushed like a puppy from one to the other of us, then she dashed in among the flocks of flamingos, retrieved a duck we had shot, and finally went swimming in the lake, where one of us had to cover her with a rifle on account of the crocodiles. Later, when we passed a herd of camels, I was obliged to put her on the chain; this made her furious and her efforts to meet these new friends nearly pulled my arms off. I, however, had no wish to see a stampeding, panic-stricken herd of camels falling over each other, bellowing, gurgling, legs intertwined, and Elsa in their midst. Fortunately, these were the last livestock we met along the shore.

When night fell we saw the fires of the camp by the lake. Again I put Elsa on the chain for fear that she might have enough energy left to chase our donkeys. When we arrived we found camp already pitched and everything laid out for dinner. While we had a belated sundowner we decided that at dawn each morning the lion party— George and I, Nuru, a Game Scout as guide, and Elsa—would start off, while camp was being struck and the animals saddled and loaded. In this way, we would benefit by the cooler hours and the pack animals would follow at a safe distance, dispensing us from any need to keep Elsa on the chain. Then about nine-thirty we would look for a shady place where we could rest during the heat of the day and where the donkeys could get some grazing. As soon as these were sighted, we would put Elsa on the chain. In the afternoon we would reverse our routine, the donkey party leaving two hours before the lion party and pitching camp before dark. We kept to this routine during the whole safari and it worked out very well, for it kept Elsa and the donkeys apart, except during the midday rest, when she was chained up and very sleepy. As it turned out, both parties soon learned to take each other for granted and to accept that everything which formed part of the safari must be tolerated.

We passed a chain of camels

Elsa trotted seven or eight hours daily

We found that Elsa marched well until about nine in the morning, then she began to feel the heat and kept stopping wherever a rock or bush gave shade. In the afternoon she was reluctant to move before five; after that, once her pads had hardened, she could have gone on all night. On an average she trotted from seven to eight hours daily, and kept in wonderful condition. She dipped herself in the lake and swam as often as possible, often only six or eight feet from the crocodiles; no shouting or waving on my part would bring her back till she felt like coming. Usually we reached camp between eight and nine in the evening; often the donkey party would fire Very lights to guide us.

The second day out we left the last human habitation behind us; it was a small fishing village of the primitive El Molo tribe. This tribe numbers about eighty souls who live almost entirely on fish, varied occasionally by crocodile and hippo meat. As a result of this badly balanced diet and of interbreeding many of them are deformed and show signs of rickets. Perhaps also owing to malnutrition, or, more likely, to the fact that the lake water contains a high proportion of natron and other minerals, they also suffer from bad teeth and gums.

They are a friendly and generous people, and a stranger is always welcomed with a gift of fresh fish. Their fishing is mostly carried on by means of nets, which they make out of doum-palm fiber, the only fiber that does not rot in the alkaline water; while the giant Nile perch, which runs up to two hundred pounds and over, and crocodile and hippo, are harpooned from rafts made from three palm logs lashed roughly together. These unwieldy craft are poled along in the shallows and never venture far out for fear of the violent winds which often sweep the lake and sometimes attain a velocity of over ninety miles an hour. Indeed, it is the wind which makes life thoroughly un-

comfortable for any traveller in this region. It is impossible to pitch a tent; food is either blown out of the plate before one can eat it, or so covered with grit as to be inedible. Sleep is almost impossible because of the tearing gusts which fill eyes, nose and ears with sand and almost lift up the bed. Yet, in spite of these torments, the lake has real beauty in its quieter moments, and exercises a fascination difficult to describe, which makes one want to return again and again.

A gift of fresh fish

The first ten days took us along its shore. The country around was grim: lava, and more lava, only the consistency of the lava differed. Sometimes it was cinder-fine dust, at others sharp-edged so that our feet became sore from slipping and sliding over the uneven ground. In certain places there was deep sand, and as we waded along each step was an effort. Or again, we had to make our way across coarse grit or pebbles and at all times the hot wind blew, sapping our energy and making us feel dizzy. There was little vegetation, only a few thorny meager plants, which pricked, and razor-edged grass, which cut the skin.

To keep Elsa's paws in good condition, I had often to grease them, an act which she seemed to understand and to like. During the midday rest I usually lay on my camp bed so as to be able to relax in more comfort than the hard pebbles provided. Elsa saw the point of this, adopted my idea, and joined me. Soon I could consider myself fortunate if she left me a small corner, and sometimes I was unlucky and

Elsa shared my camp bed

Elsa tantalized by the sight of the donkeys

had to sit on the ground while she stretched herself full-length on the bed. But as a rule we curled up together on the bed, I hoping that it might not break beneath our combined weight. During our long marches Nuru always carried drinking water and a bowl for Elsa; she had her evening meal toward nine o'clock and afterward slept heavily, tied up near my bed.

One evening we lost our way and were guided by Very lights to the camp, which we reached late at night. Elsa seemed exhausted, so I left her unchained to recover; but although she looked sleepy she suddenly rushed at full speed to the thorn enclosure in which the donkeys spent the night, and crashed through the fence in real feline style. Braying, panic, and pandemonium ensued, and before we could intervene all the donkeys had bolted into the darkness. Luckily, we soon caught Elsa and I gave her a good hiding. She seemed to understand that she deserved it and, as far as she could, showed that she was sorry. I felt guilty at having underestimated her natural instinct and the tremendous

Game Scouts offer a catfish to Elsa

temptation that a nice-smelling donkey herd must be to her, especially at an hour when the hunting spirit is most alive in wild animals.

Luckily, only one poor donkey had received scratches and these were not serious. I dressed them and they soon healed, but this episode was a warning to me never to leave her unguarded.

Fish were plentiful and as a rule George and Julian were able to keep the camp supplied with delicious fish called giant *tilapia*, a *spécialité* unique to Lake Rudolf. These they caught by either rod or line, or by stunning them with a rifle bullet. The Game Scouts seemed to prefer the ugly-looking catfish which lay in the shallows and which they were able to kill with sticks and stones. Elsa was always ready to join in the fun, and sometimes she would retrieve a catfish, soon to drop it and wrinkle her nose in disgust. One day we saw Nuru, who always carried a shotgun, lifting it up by the barrel and clubbing a catfish with it. He did this with such force that the stock split through in many places, broke, and projected at right angles to the barrel. Nuru was so delighted with his catfish that he was quite oblivious to the damage he had done. When George pointed it out to him, he replied calmly: "Oh, Mungo [God] will help you to get another gun." Elsa, however, took her revenge, for she ran off with Nuru's sandals, which he had left on the shore, and galloped away with them; it was a funny sight to watch the two trying to outwit each other. In the end, the sandals were in poor shape when their owner got them back.

Before we reached Alia Bay some hundred miles to the north it was necessary to cross the long Longondoti range. In several places the hills fall straight into the lake, so the donkeys with their bulky loads had to make a detour inland, while the lion party struggled across the rocks and kept to the shore. At one point we looked like being defeated by a difficult corner, for here Elsa, to wade around the point, had the choice of either jumping down a fifteen-foot cliff, covered with a slippery deposit on which it was impossible for her to get any grip, to land in the shallow water below, or of scrambling down an equally steep rock to land in the foaming waters which crashed

93

against its foot. The water was in fact only about her own depth, but the foam made it look very dangerous and she did not know what to do. She tried every ledge of the rock, padding desperately on her small platform, till bravely she jumped into the lashing waves and finally, coaxed by us, soon reached dry ground. It was touching to see how delighted and proud she was of her achievement and also at having pleased us.

For most of the way we had to drink and to cook with brackish lake water which, although harmless and so soft that it is beautiful for bathing and does not need soap for washing, has a disagreeable taste and tainted all our food. So it was indeed a pleasant surprise to find a little spring of fresh water at the foot of the hills called Moiti.

The route we took along the western foot of these hills had, so far as we knew, never before been travelled by a European; the few who had visited this region in the past had kept well to the east. Nine days out of Loyongalane, we camped at the northern end of the hills. As usual, we had sent a party of Game Scouts ahead to spy out the country and keep a lookout for poachers. Early in the afternoon they returned and reported seeing a large body of men in canoes. The only tribe on the lake which possesses proper dugout canoes is the Galubba, a turbulent people, well supplied with rifles, who constantly carry out raids from across the Ethiopian border into our territory, looting and murdering. The band which the Scouts had seen might be either a raiding party or a poaching and fishing expedition. In any case, they had no right to be there. Elsa and I remained in camp, with four Game Scouts armed with rifles to protect us, while the rest of the party went off to reconnoiter.

When they had reached the top of a ridge which overlooked the bay, they saw three canoes with twelve men on board, close inshore, paddling in the direction of our camp. However, they at once spotted our party, so that by the time George and the other men had reached the water's edge the canoes were a good two hundred yards out, making for a small island and paddling madly. They did not appear to have

Elsa reluctant to leap from the ledge

firearms, though, of course, they might have had rifles concealed in the canoes. Looking through glasses, George saw a body of at least forty men on the island and several canoes drawn up on its shore. He watched the canoes reach the beach and an obviously excited group gather around them. Then—since without a boat there was nothing much that they could do—the party returned to camp. We packed up at once and moved to the bay below, as close as possible to the island. That night, extra sentries were posted and every man slept with his rifle, loaded, beside him. When dawn broke, we saw that the island was deserted. Evidently the Galubba had not liked the look of us and had decided to get away during the hours of darkness, in spite of a heavy gale which had blown up during the night. To make sure that they really had gone, George sent patrols along the shore. Soon after sunup we saw a multitude of vultures and marabous descending upon the island; this led us to suppose that the Galubba had been on a poaching and fishing expedition and had no doubt killed several hippos, on the remains of which the vultures and storks had come to feast.

At about eleven in the morning two canoes suddenly issued out of a dense belt of reeds, to the south of the camp, and made for open water. To discourage them, George put a few bullets across their bows, which sent them back into the reeds in a hurry. He then sent some Scouts to try to make contact with the Galubba and persuade them to come ashore. But, although the Scouts managed to get within hailing distance, the poachers would not respond and retreated farther into the swamp. Throughout the day, we could see their heads bobbing above the reeds to inspect us. We estimated that there were four canoes in the reeds, probably stragglers from the main body. Since it was impossible to reach them, George thought the next best thing was to encourage them to make for home, so as soon as it was dark he fired tracer bullets and a few Very lights at intervals over the swamp.

By now our supplies were running low and it was time to turn back. As it turned out, the first part of the safari was luxury compared to the second because we had had plenty of water from the lake. Now, instead of retracing our steps, we decided to take an inland route. Goite, our Turkana guide, did not seem very sure of the way and, what was worse, was not certain whether we should find water when needed. For the region was dependent on waterholes, which at this dry season were few and far between. George, however, calculated that we should never be more than a long day's march from the lake so, if pressed for water, we could make for it. We missed the cooling breeze off the lake, and there were times when I felt nearly dehydrated by the heat. The country here was even more desolate than the one we had passed through on our outward march. There was nothing but lava, so, understandably, there was little game and no population. Luckily, we had bought sheep at Loyongalane, and though Elsa's living larder was rapidly dwindling away it was sufficient to solve her feeding problem. But all of us lost most of our surplus weight during this time. Our march back was rapid, because the donkeys were now carrying less weight and, much of the route being waterless, we had to do longer marches.

A rare and welcome water hole

When after eighteen days we got back to Loyongalane we found that the Scouts we had left behind to protect our base had not been idle. They produced four Turkana poachers, who had been caught trapping game. The oldest greeted George with great affection and reminded him that, some ten years ago, he had caught him committing the same offense and had sent him to jail at Marsabit. He said that he had quite enjoyed his enforced stay there but did not wish to repeat it. Owing to his age, George relented and, unofficially, sentenced him to be donkey driver for the rest of the safari.

From Loyongalane the men went to North Horr, where there were three Somali shops, to buy food for the Africans. At the police station George learned from the African Inspector in Charge that a gang of eight mounted poachers armed with rifles had been seen between Loyongalane and North Horr. These poachers are usually Boran tribesmen from across the border. Mounted on ponies which have been trained to go without water for four or even five days, and often armed with rifles, they ride down and shoot giraffe. They are harbored by their compatriots on our side of the border, who give them prompt warning of approaching patrols. However, in this case, a camel patrol had followed the raiders' tracks for several days, finally surprised them, wounded one man, and captured seven ponies.

We spent three days at Loyongalane, refitting, mending saddlery, etc., in preparation for the second part of our safari, the ascent of Mount Kulal. This mountain, which lies twenty miles east of the lake, rises out of the surrounding desert to about seventy-five hundred feet; it catches all the moisture from the monsoon on its upper levels and has developed a rich forest on its summit. It is a narrow volcano, twenty-eight miles long, with a crater in the center about four miles wide. This crater is split in half and divides the mountain into a southern and a northern portion. There is a theory that, after the volcano became extinct, an earthquake broke Kulal into deep crevasses, and cracked the awe-inspiring fissure through the crater. Its smooth walls are split like the peel of an orange when it is cut. These deep ridges fall three

99

A Turkana Tribal Policeman

thousand feet from the crater's lip. At the bottom, invisible from the top, is a gorge called Il Sigata which leads into the heart of the mountain. Its sheer walls tower hundreds of feet high and the opening is in places so narrow that the sky above is visible only through a slit. We tried to explore the gorge, entering it from the only accessible opening, which lies toward the eastern foot of Kulal, but we were defeated after a few hours by huge rocks and deep waterpools which blocked the way.

To cover the mountain thoroughly it was necessary to go up one half, down again to the bottom, and then up the second part.

The object of the safari was to find out whether the game on the mountain was holding its own, or decreasing as a result of poaching, by comparing the present situation with that found by George when twelve years previously he had last visited the area. In particular, we wanted to investigate the state of the greater kudu.

Kulal does not look impressive from below: a long stretching mountain, with broad ridges leading to its summit; as we were to discover, these ridges became so narrow that the approaches for pack animals are very limited.

The first day's march, over thickly strewn lava boulders, was extremely arduous for laden animals. Later the ascent up knife-edged ridges was, in many places, very difficult to negotiate and we found it necessary to off-load the donkeys and manhandle the loads.

On the second night we were two-thirds of the way up the mountain and camped in a precipitous valley choked with lava boulders, near a little spring which provided just sufficient water for one animal at a time. It was very late before the last donkey had its much needed drink. This was one of the few waterholes on Kulal, and so it was naturally a vital center for the Samburu tribesmen who bring their livestock up to Kulal in the dry season.

It must have been difficult for Elsa to meet these large herds of camels, cattle, goats, and sheep around this and other waterholes; but she was intelligent and good-natured and, apparently realizing what

However thirsty, Elsa always waited her turn

the situation was, she put up with the tantalizing smell of these animals which often passed within a few feet of her. On these occasions we put her on the chain but she made no attempt to attack and only wanted to get away from the dust and the noise.

The route up Kulal was steep and the climate became arctic as we reached the higher slopes. We walked over saddles, crossed deep ravines, and struggled along precipices. Here the bush was lower and then it changed into beautiful alpine flora.

Next morning we reached the top of Kulal; it was a relief to be walking on more or less even ground. Camp was pitched in a beautiful little glade, close to a rather muddy spring, fouled by the cattle of the Samburu tribesmen. Their astonishment was great at finding a nearly fully grown lion in our camp.

In the dense forest belt near the top on most mornings there was heavy mist, so we made a blazing cedar-log fire to keep us warm. At night it was so cold that I kept Elsa in my small tent, made her a nest of lichen, and covered her with my warmest blanket. Most of my night was usually spent replacing it as it fell off continually and Elsa would begin to shiver. When I did this, she always licked my arm. She never made any attempt to tear the tent and get out; on the contrary, she remained in it long after her usual waking hour, snuggling in her nest,

where she was warm and cozy, whereas outside there was a blasting gale and wet mist. But as soon as the sun had cleared the fog away, she came to life and enjoyed the invigorating mountain air. Indeed, she loved the place, for the ground was soft and cool, the forest gave thick shade, and there were plenty of buffalo droppings to roll in.

Because of the shade and altitude, walking during the heat of the day was no effort in this region, and she was able to explore the mountain with us. She watched the eagles circling high in the air and was annoyed by the crows who followed her and dived low to tease her, and on one occasion she woke a buffalo out of his sleep and chased him. She had excellent scent, hearing, and eyesight and never lost herself in the thick undergrowth. One afternoon we were following the advance party, which had gone well ahead through the forest, and Elsa was ambushing us in a playful way from behind every bush, when suddenly, from the direction in which she had just disappeared, we heard a panic-stricken bray. A moment later a donkey broke through the wood with Elsa clinging to it and mauling it. Fortunately, the forest was so thick that they could not go very fast, so we quickly reached the struggling pair and gave Elsa the beating we thought she deserved. She had never done anything of this sort before, and I was very much alarmed, for I had prided myself on the fact that she always obeyed my call instead of chasing an animal unduly. But again I could only blame myself for not putting Elsa on the lead, and the donkey herdsman who had let the animal stray behind the others. It was an unfortunate coincidence that while being loaded on this particular day the donkeys had behaved most provocatively to Elsa, walking close to her while she was chained up. No doubt, later when roaming through the forest she found one poor donkey alone, it proved too much of a temptation for her. In addition, this donkey was old and had given us a lot of trouble during the safari. So taking everything into consideration, I was tempted to forgive rather than to blame Elsa, when she pleaded so touchingly for forgiveness and tried out every one of her tricks to win back our good opinion.

103

A Samburu girl

One day we stood on the lip of the crater which divides the mountain and looked across to the northern part, which was not more than four miles distant, though we knew that it would take us a full two days' march to get there. Nonchalantly Elsa balanced herself on the edge of the two-thousand-foot precipice, a sight which nearly sent me into hysterics. But animals seem to have no fear of heights. The following day we descended and the safari reached the mouth of the great Il Sigata gorge; there we made camp.

During the day thousands of camels, goats, and sheep herded by tall, good-looking Rendille tribesmen passed by on their way to water four miles up the gorge. They were followed by women leading strings of camels tied nose to tail loaded with water containers. These held about six gallons each and were made of closely woven fiber. We walked up the cleft, or rather, literally *into* the mountain. The floor of the gorge is a dry watercourse which, for about five miles, rises gently between towering walls which climb sharply on each side; when one penetrates still farther these walls attain some fifteen hundred feet in height and are sheer precipice. In places the gorge is so narrow that two laden camels cannot pass abreast and the cliffs overhang, shutting out the sky. We went far beyond the watering place of the stock, where the trickle of water becomes a sizable brook, with many rock-bound pools of clear water. Finally we were halted by a sheer fall of thirty feet. Herbert, who is a mountaineer, managed to get up it only to find another high fall beyond.

Il Sigata used to be a favorite place for poachers because it was easy to lie in wait for animals going to water. In fact, once an animal had entered the trap it was doomed, since there was no way out except that which led past the waiting hunters.

From Il Sigata it was a day and a half's march to the top of the northern massif, which we found to be more thickly inhabited by the Samburu and their livestock than the southern part. So Elsa's liberty had here to be curtailed.

We saw little game. Buffalo, of which there used to be a lot, had

105

Elsa rested in a tree to catch the breeze

Elsa at Lake Rudolf

not, we were told, visited the northern end of the mountain for the last six years. There were also no greater kudu to be seen, though we observed the spoor of a few. George considered that this absence of game was probably due to the great number of Samburu stock which were eating up the grazing and rapidly denuding the mountain.

Owing to sharp broken lava, the descent to Loyongalane was a most exhausting struggle, and not even the superb view of Lake Rudolf far below, reflecting the setting sun in its lead-colored surface against deep indigo hills and an orange-yellow sky, could compensate us for our tumbles, which grew more and more frequent.

Elsa kept looking back at the mountain and cool forest and started to run toward them, so we had to put her on the chain.

Toward nightfall we lost our way in the dark. Elsa lay down every few yards, making it very plain that she had had enough. Although she was nearly full-grown, she still liked to suck my thumb when she felt nervous, and there was a lot of thumb-sucking that night. At last some tracer bullets, fired by the advance party, guided us to the camp. When we staggered in after our nightmare march, Elsa refused food and only wanted to be near me. I also could not eat from exhaustion and could well imagine the effort it had cost Elsa to carry on. She, of course, could not know why we were doing such a senseless thing as to struggle across sharp lava at night, and it was only her affection for us and her trust that kept her going. In spite of the hardships she had endured on this safari, in the course of which she had walked well over three hundred miles, the bond between us had only been strengthened. As long as she was with us and knew herself to be loved and secure, she was happy. To feel that we were responsible for such a proud, intelligent animal, who had no other living creature to satisfy her strongly developed need for affection and her gregarious instincts, attached us all the more deeply to her. Sometimes, it is true, she was unwittingly a nuisance; for instance, because we could not leave her in care of anyone else, we became to some extent her prisoners, but she gave us so much in return for these small sacrifices. The difference

between her reactions and ours came only from her natural charac-
teristics intended to be developed and used in the normal life of a
wild lion. It was very touching to watch her trying to control the
strong forces within her and to adapt herself to our way of life in order
to please us. Her good-natured temperament was certainly due in part
to her character, but part too may have come from the fact that neither
force nor frustration was ever used to adapt her to our way of life.
For we tried by kindness alone to help her to overcome the differences
that lie between our two worlds.

In natural life, as long as he finds food, a lion does not wander over
great distances, and certainly Elsa had seen more of the world than she
would have done living with a pride. Yet she knew her home, and
whenever we returned from safari she would go straight back to her
habits and usual routine.

Elsa and Wild Lions

E L S A has charming manners; no matter for how short a time we have been separated, she will greet us ceremoniously, walking from one to the other, rubbing her head against us while miaowing in a low moan. Invariably, I come first, then George, followed by Nuru, and whoever happens to be near is afterward greeted in the same way. She knows at once who likes her and reacts affectionately. She tolerates justifiably nervous guests, but those who are really scared have a hard time. Not that she has ever done them any harm, but she delights in thoroughly terrifying them.

Since she was a tiny cub she has known just how to use her weight. By now it had become much more effective. Whenever she wanted to stop us, she flung herself with all her force at our feet, pressing her body against our shins and thus knocking us over.

Soon after our return from Lake Rudolf when we took her out for her evening walks she began to display a growing restlessness. Sometimes she refused to return with us, and she spent the night out in the bush. Usually we succeeded in getting her back by going to fetch her in the Land Rover. In fact, she soon decided that it was a waste of energy to walk home when a car had been specially brought to fetch her. So she would jump onto the canvas roof and loll at her ease, and from this vantage point she could watch out for game as we drove along. This was a very satisfactory arrangement from her point of view but, unfortunately, the manufacturers had not designed the roof as a couch for a lioness. As a result the supports began to give way

For short rides Elsa preferred the roof of the Land Rover

under the strain and we found Elsa gradually subsiding on top of us. So George had to rig up extra supports and reinforce the canvas.

When she was not with us, Nuru was still always in charge of Elsa; one day we wanted to film him with her and told him that he should wear something rather smarter than his usual tattered shirt and trousers. In a few minutes he reappeared in a startling, close-fitting cream-colored jacket, with braid and frogging down the front, which he had bought for his wedding. We thought that he looked just like a professional lion tamer in it. Elsa took one look at him and made at once for the bush; from there she peeped out from behind a shrub until she had established his identity. Then she came up to him and gave him a smack as though to say: "What the devil do you mean by giving me such a fright?"

Nuru and Elsa had many adventures together. For instance, one day Nuru told us that while they were resting under a bush a leopard approached them downwind. Elsa watched eagerly and, although tense with excitement, kept still and controlled herself, except for her tail, until the leopard was nearly on top of her. Then suddenly the animal noticed the switching tail and bolted like lightning, nearly overrunning Nuru in its flight.

Elsa was now twenty-three months old, and her voice broke to a deep growl. A month later she seemed to be in season again and placed her jets on many bushes, no doubt as an invitation to a mate. Normally she followed us on our walks wherever we went, but now for two days she had seemed determined to cross the valley. On this particular afternoon, she led us in *her* direction, and we soon found the fresh pugmarks of a lion. At dark, she refused to return. As we were near a car track, we went back to get the Land Rover, and George set off in it while I stayed at home in case she took a short cut back. When he reached the place where we had left her, George shouted to her for some time, but there was no response—only the hills echoed his calls. . . . He drove on for another mile, calling at intervals. Then, hoping that Elsa had already come home, he returned. I told him I had

Elsa's pugmarks

waited for two long hours, but that there was still no sign of her, so he left again and some time after he had gone I heard a shot. Until he came back I was very anxious, and then most upset by what he had to tell me.

He had driven out and called for a good half hour, but Elsa had not shown up. Then he had stopped the car in an opening in the bush, wondering where to look next. Suddenly, some two hundred yards behind the car there had been a great uproar of lions quarrelling. Then, the next moment a lioness flashed by with another in hot pursuit. As they shot past, George seized his rifle and put a bullet under the second animal, assuming, probably rightly, that she was a jealous lioness, bent on Elsa's destruction. Then he jumped into the car and gave chase. He drove along a narrow lane between dense thornbush, flashing a spot-light from side to side, until he was brought up short by a lion and two lionesses, who only very reluctantly moved out of his way, giving vent to loud roars.

Now he had come to fetch me; we drove back to the scene, but though we called desperately for Elsa—called and called—no familiar sound came in answer. But presently, as if in derision, the lion chorus started up a few hundred yards away. We drove toward them until we could see the glint of three pairs of eyes. There was nothing more to be done. So, with heavy hearts, we turned for home. Would Elsa be killed by a jealous lioness? In her present condition, she might easily have mated with the lion, and it was a question whether his lioness would tolerate a rival. However, to our great relief, we had not gone more than a mile along the track when we came upon Elsa, sniffing at a bush. She utterly ignored us. We tried to persuade her to join us but she remained where we had found her, gazing wistfully into the bush in the direction in which the lions had last been heard. Presently they started calling again, and approached. Thirty yards behind us was a dry river bed, and here the pride stopped, growling vigorously.

It was now well after midnight. Elsa sat in the moonlight between the lions and us, both parties calling her to their side. Who was going to win the contest? Suddenly Elsa moved toward the lions and I shouted, "Elsa, *no*, don't go there, you'll get killed." She sat down again, looking at us and looking back at her own kind, undecided what to do. For an hour the situation did not alter, then George fired two shots over the lions; this had the effect of sending them off in silence. Then, as Elsa had still not made up her mind, we drove slowly back, hoping that she might follow us; and so she did. Very reluctantly, she walked parallel with the car, looking back many times, till finally she hopped onto the roof and we brought her back to safety. When we arrived home she was very thirsty and exhausted and drank without stopping.

What had happened during the five hours which Elsa had spent with the lions? Would a wild pride accept her in spite of the human smell which she carried? Would a male ignore a female in season? Why had she returned with us instead of joining her own kind? Was it because she was frightened of the fierce lioness? These were some of the questions we asked ourselves. The fact remained that she had come to no harm as a result of this experience.

A pride of two lions

But after this adventure the call of the wild evidently grew stronger and stronger. Often she did not return with us at dark, and we spent many evenings looking for her. In the dry season water was our main hold on her, for this she could get only at the house.

Rocks were her favorite places, and she always chose the top of a cliff or some other safe position as her lookout. Once, in spite of hearing a leopard "coughing" close by, we had to leave her on such a rock. Next morning she returned with several bleeding scratches, and we wondered whether the leopard was responsible for them.

Another time, after sunset, she followed the laughing cries of a hyena; soon these increased to hysterical shrieks to which Elsa replied by loud growls. George rushed to see what was happening and was just in time to shoot one of two hyenas, which were closing in on Elsa. After this she pulled her "kill" into a bush, dragging it between her front legs as she had often done with a ground sheet when she was a cub. But, although she was now two years old, her teeth could not yet penetrate the skin of a hyena, and she did not know what to do with her quarry.

The river bed was an ideal training ground

Elsa on her rock

At this age giraffes still remained her favorite friends. She would stalk them, using every stratagem of her kind, but invariably they would spot her before she got too close; this was mainly because Elsa seemed unable to control her tail. Her body would freeze without so much as the twitch of an ear, but the conspicuous black tassel on her tail would never keep still. Once the giraffes had spotted her, there would be a competition to see who would be the boldest among them. One by one, in a half-circle, they would edge forward, giving vent to low, long-drawn snorts, until Elsa could contain herself no longer and would make a rush and put the herd to flight. On two occasions she made a sustained chase after a huge old bull; only after they had gone about a mile the giraffe, either winded or fed up with being chased, turned at bay. Elsa then circled him closely, keeping just out of reach of the mighty pounding forelegs, a blow from which could easily have smashed her skull.

She seemed to come into season every two and a half months. We had been told that the most obvious indication of this condition

Elsa with Nuru, Makedde, and the driver Ibrahim

was a loud purring; although she had by now been twice in season we had never noticed anything of the kind, but each time she had a peculiar smell and sprayed her invitation jets on the bushes.

Soon after her adventure with the lions Nuru reported that, when in the morning he tried to follow her, Elsa had growled at him repeatedly. Obviously she wished him to remain behind, while she walked determinedly into the hills. So, in spite of the increasing heat, she had trotted off quickly until he lost her tracks in the rocks. In the afternoon we followed her spoor, but soon lost it and could only call to her from the foot of the cliffs. A reply came, a strange growl, unlike Elsa's voice but undoubtedly that of a lion. Soon afterward we saw her struggling downhill, over the boulders, calling in her familiar way. When she reached us she flung herself exhausted onto the ground, panting and very excited. We had brought water with us and she could not have enough of it. Now we noticed several bleeding claw marks on her hind legs, shoulders, and neck and also two

118

Elsa's exercises to strengthen her claws

bleeding perforations on her forehead, which were definitely made by teeth and not by claws.[1]

Although normally she had no personal smell, she now certainly had a very strong one, much stronger than her present seasonal smell. As soon as she had recovered a little, she greeted us in her customary manner, as well as purring at each of us in turn in a most startling way, as though to say: "Listen to what I have learned."

When she had assured herself of our admiration, she threw herself on the ground again and fell fast asleep for two hours. She had obviously just been with a lion when we had interfered by calling to her.

Two days later she spent a whole day and night away, and when we followed her spoor we found her in the company of a lioness, both having laid up several times together.

From this time onward, Elsa spent more and more nights away. We tried to induce her to come home by driving near to her favorite places and calling to her. Occasionally she came, more often she did not. Sometimes she was away, without food or water, for two or three days. Water was still some hold over her, but soon the rains were due and we realized that when they came we should lose all control of her. This raised a problem which we had to solve; it was one which was made more urgent by the fact that our long overseas leave was due in May. Elsa was now twenty-seven months old, almost full-grown. We had always known that we could not keep her free indefinitely at Isiolo. Our original idea had been to send her to join her sisters at the Rotterdam Zoo, and we had even made the necessary arrangements in case an emergency should arise. But now she had taken her future into her own paws, and her latest developments were decisive in altering our plans for her. Because we had been so fortunate in bringing her up in her natural environment and because she seemed so much at home in the bush and was accepted by wild animals, we felt that she might well

[1] Is it a coincidence that when two years later I visited the Rome Zoo on my way to London, I saw a couple of lions mating and as the last gesture of the siring act, the male bit the lioness on the forehead? Soon afterward I saw the same action take place in the same circumstances in the London Zoo.

Elsa's grimace at a new scent

prove to be the exception to the rule that a pet will be killed by its own kind because of its human smell and ignorance of bush life. To release Elsa back to the wild would be an experiment well worth trying.

We intended to spend two or three weeks with her, then, if all went well, we would take our long leave; one is supposed to spend this outside Kenya, in order to have a change of climate.

Next we had to consider *where* to release Elsa. Unfortunately, Isiolo was far too populated for us to let her go wild there. But we knew of an area which for most of the year was devoid of inhabitants and livestock but had an abundance of game, especially lion.

We received permission to take Elsa to this place and made the necessary arrangements. The rains were expected any day, so we had no time to lose, if she were to reach her possible future home before they began.

Elsa rolls in elephant droppings

Sleepy or bored?

In order to get to this area we should have to travel three hundred and forty miles, crossing the highlands on our way and also the Great Rift Valley, going through relatively thickly populated country where there were many European farms. Because we feared that Elsa might be embarrassed by gaping crowds and inquisitive Africans at every halt, and also to avoid the heat of the day, we decided to travel by night. We settled to start about seven in the evening, but Elsa had other ideas. Before setting off we took her out for her usual walk to her favorite rocks, across the valley from our house. There I photographed her for the last time in her home. She is genuinely camera-shy and always hates being filmed or sketched. As soon as she sees one of those awful shiny boxes focused on her she invariably turns her head, or covers it with a paw, or just walks away. On this last day at Isiolo she had to endure a lot from our Leica and plainly got thoroughly fed up with it. So finally she took her revenge. When, for a moment, I left the camera unguarded, she leapt up, sprang upon it, and galloped away with it over the rocks. That, we thought, was the end of our precious Leica. For more than an hour we tried every device to rescue it, but as we tried each new trick we had invented for the purpose, she shook it more provokingly between her teeth, or chewed at it, holding it firmly between her paws. Finally we recovered it, and miraculously it was not badly damaged.

By then it was time to get back to the house and start off on the long journey, but just then Elsa sat herself on a rock and gazed across the valley in the contemplative manner of her kind and nothing would move her. Obviously she had no intention of walking back and expected the car to be brought for her. All hope of making an early start was gone. George went home, fetched the car, and came back to the foot of the hills where we had left Elsa, but she was no longer there and had apparently gone for her evening stroll. He called to her, but there was no response. Not until eleven at night did she reappear, jump onto the roof of the Land Rover, and consent to be driven home.

Last day at Isiolo

The First Release

I t was after midnight when we had at last secured Elsa in her travelling crate and started off. In the hope of making the trip easier for her I gave her a tranquillizer; we had been told by the vet that the drug was harmless and that the effect would last about eight hours. To give Elsa all the moral support I could, I travelled with her in the open truck. During the night we passed through country that is eight thousand feet above sea level, and the cold was icy. Owing to the effect of the tranquillizer Elsa was only semiconscious, yet even in this state every few minutes she stretched her paws out through the bars of the crate, to assure herself that I was still there. It took us seventeen hours to reach our destination. The effect of the tranquillizer did not wear off until an hour after we had arrived. During these eighteen hours Elsa became very cold, her breathing was slow, and for a time I feared that she was going to die. Luckily, she recovered, but this experience showed us that one should be very careful with drugs where lions are concerned, for they are far more sensitive to them than other animals and individually they react differently. We had had previous experience of this when we had powdered all three cubs with an insecticide—one took it well, one became sick, and Elsa was very ill with convulsions.

It was late in the afternoon by the time we reached our destination; there we were met by a friend who is the Game Warden of this district. We pitched camp on a superb site at the base of a thousand-foot escarpment overlooking a vast plain of open bush country, through which a belt of dark vegetation marks the course of a river. As we were at an altitude of five thousand feet, the air was fresh and brisk. Immediately in front of our camp lay open grassland sloping toward the plain, on which herds of Thomson's gazelle, topi, wildebeest, Burchell's zebra, roan antelope, kongoni, and a few buffalo were grazing. It was a game paradise. While the tents were being pitched we took Elsa for a stroll and she rushed at the herds, not knowing which to follow, for in every direction there were animals running. As if to shake off the effects of the ghastly journey, Elsa lost herself among these new playmates, who were rather astonished to find such a strange lion in their midst; one who rushed foolishly to and fro without any apparent purpose. Soon, however, Elsa had had enough and trotted back to camp and her dinner.

Our plan was this: we would spend the first week taking Elsa, perched on the roof of the Land Rover, around the new country, thus getting her used to it and to the animals, many of which belonged to species which do not live in the Northern Frontier and she had therefore never seen. During the second week we intended to leave her overnight, while she was active in the bush, and to visit and feed her in the mornings when she was sleepy. Afterward we would reduce her meals, in the hope that this would encourage her to kill on her own, or to join a wild lion.

On the morning after our arrival we started our program. First we took off her collar, as the symbol of liberation. Elsa hopped onto the roof of the Land Rover and we went off. After only a few hundred yards we saw a lioness walking parallel to us down hill; she passed close to many antelope who took no notice of her, realizing no doubt from her determined steady stride that at the moment she was not interested in killing. We drove closer to the lioness. Elsa displayed much excitement, jumped off her seat, and, making low moaning noises, cautiously followed this new friend. But as soon as the lioness stopped and turned around, her courage failed her and she raced back as fast as she could to the safety of the car. The lioness continued her purposeful walk, and we soon detected six cubs waiting for her on a small ant-hill in tall grass.

We drove on and surprised a hyena chewing a bone. Elsa jumped off and chased the startled animal, who had only time to grasp her bone and lumber away. In spite of her ungainliness, she made good her escape but lost her bone in the process.

Later we passed through herd after herd of different antelope, whose curiosity seemed to be aroused by the sight of a Land Rover with a lion on it and allowed us, provided that we remained in the car and did not talk, to approach within a few yards of them. All the time Elsa watched carefully but did not attempt to leave the car unless she spotted an animal off guard, grazing with its back toward her, or fighting; then she would get down quietly and creep forward with her belly close to the ground, taking advantage of every bit of cover, and thus advance toward her victim. But as soon as the animal showed any suspicion, she either froze to immobility or, if the situation seemed better handled in another way, she pretended to be uninterested, licked her paws, yawned, or even rolled on her back, until the animal was reassured. Then she would at once start stalking again. But however cunning she was, she never got close enough to kill.

The little Thomson's gazelles provoked Elsa, very unfairly, relying on the unwritten law of the bush that a superior creature will not attack a smaller one, except for food. They are the real urchins of the plain, most inquisitive and always busy with their tails. Now they challenged her, teased her, and simply asked to be chased; but Elsa only looked bored, ignored them, and with dignity put them in their place.

Buffaloes and rhinos were quite another matter. They *had* to be chased. One day, from the car, we watched a buffalo cantering across the plain. Perhaps his curiosity was aroused by seeing a lion on the Land Rover. Quickly Elsa jumped to the ground and, using the cover of a bush, set out to stalk him. The buffalo had the same idea and also used this cover but starting from the opposite direction. We

*Elsa meets some **Thomson's** gazelles*

waited, and watched, until we saw them nearly collide. Then it was the buffalo who bolted, with Elsa bravely following him.

On another occasion, from her seat on the Land Rover she saw two buffaloes asleep in a bush. Off she went; bellows, crashing, and a wild commotion followed, then the buffaloes broke through the thicket and galloped away in different directions.

Rhinos too were most inviting; one day we came upon one standing fast asleep with its head buried in a bush. Elsa stalked him very carefully and succeeded in nearly rubbing noses with him. Then the poor beast had an abrupt awakening, gave a startled snort, and, looking bewildered, spun around on himself and dashed into a near-by swamp. There he churned up the water and gave Elsa a shower bath; she splashed on after him; outlined against high sprays of water, the pair disappeared from our sight, and it was a long time before Elsa returned, wet but proud.

She loved climbing trees, and sometimes when we had looked in vain for her in the high grass we found her swaying in the crown of a tree. More than once she had difficulty in getting down again. Once, after trying various possibilities, and making the branch she was on bend alarmingly under her weight, we saw her tail dangling through the foliage, followed by her struggling hind legs, till finally she fell onto the grass well over twenty feet below. She was most embarrassed at having lost her dignity before an audience, for, while she always enjoyed making us laugh when she meant to do so, she hated being laughed at when the joke was against her. Now she walked quickly away from us and we gave her time to regain her self-respect. When we looked for her later on, we found her holding court with six hyenas. These sinister creatures sat in a circle around her, and I felt rather nervous for her. But as though to offset her earlier clumsiness in the tree she now showed us that she was very superior to the hyenas, who bored her. She yawned, stretched herself, and, ignoring the hyenas, walked up to us. The hyenas hobbled off, looking over their shoulders, perhaps puzzled by the appearance of Elsa's strange friends.

One morning we followed circling vultures and soon found a lion on a zebra kill. He was tearing at the meat and paid no attention to us. Elsa stepped cautiously from the car, miaowing at him and then, though she did not get any encouragement, advanced carefully toward him. At last the lion looked up and straight at Elsa. He seemed to say: "Don't you know lion etiquette? How dare you, woman, interfere with the lord while he is having his meal? You are allowed to kill for me, but afterward you have to wait till I have had my lion's share, then you may finish up the remains." Evidently poor Elsa did not like his expression and returned as fast as she could to the safety of the car. The lord continued feeding and we watched him for a long time, hoping that Elsa might regain her courage; but nothing would induce her to leave her safe position.

Next morning we had better luck. We saw a topi standing, like a sentry, on an ant-hill, looking intently in one direction. We followed his glance and discovered a young lion resting in the high grass, sunning himself. He was a magnificent young male with a beautiful blond mane, and Elsa seemed attracted by him. Just the right husband for her, we thought. We drove to within thirty yards of him. The lion looked mildly surprised when he saw his prospective bride sitting on the top of a car, but responded in a friendly manner. Elsa, apparently overcome by coyness, made low moans but would not come off the roof. So we drove a little distance away and persuaded her to get down, then, suddenly, we left her and drove around to the other side of the lion: this meant that she would have to pass him in order to reach us. After much painful hesitation, she plucked up enough courage to walk toward the lion. When she was about ten paces away from him, she lay down with her ears back and her tail swishing. The lion got up and went toward her, with, I am sure, the friendliest intentions, but at the last moment Elsa panicked and rushed to the car.

We drove away with her and, strangely enough, right into a pride of two lions and one lioness on a kill.

This was luck indeed. They must have killed very recently for they were so intent upon their meal that however much Elsa talked to them they paid not the slightest attention to her. Finally they left the kill, their bulging stomachs swinging from side to side. Elsa lost no time in inspecting the remains of the carcass, her first contact with a real kill. Nothing could have served our purpose better than this meal, provided by lions and full of their fresh scent. After Elsa had had her fair share, we dragged the kill back to the handsome young lion who had seemed so friendly. We hoped that if Elsa provided him with a meal he would have a favorable opinion of her. Then we left her and the kill near to him and drove away. After a few hours we set out to see what had happened, but met Elsa already halfway back to the camp. However, since this lion had shown an interest in her, we took her back to him during the afternoon. We found him still in the same place. Elsa talked to him from her couch as though they were old friends, but had plainly no intention of leaving the car.

To induce her to quit her seat we drove behind a bush and I got out but was nearly knocked over by a hyena who dashed out of his cool retreat, in which we then found a newly killed baby zebra, no doubt provided by the blond lion. It was Elsa's feeding time, so regardless of the consequences, she jumped out of the car onto the carcass. We took this opportunity to drive away as fast as we could and left her alone for her night's adventure. Early next morning, anxious to know the outcome of the experiment, we set off to visit her, hoping to find a happy pair. What we found was poor Elsa, waiting at the spot at which we had left her, but minus the lion and minus the kill. She was overjoyed to see us, desperate to stay with us, and sucked my thumbs frantically to make sure that everything was all right between us. I was very unhappy that I had hurt her feelings without being able to explain to her that all we had done was intended to be for her good. When she had calmed down and even felt safe enough in our company to fall asleep, we decided, rather sadly, that we must break faith with her again, and we sneaked away.

Till now we had always given her her meat already cut up, so that she should not associate her food with living animals. Now we needed to reverse our system, so during her midday sleep we drove sixty miles to shoot a small buck for her. We had to go this distance because no one was allowed to shoot game near the camp. We brought her a complete buck wondering if she would know how to open it, since she had had no mother to teach her the proper way of doing it. We soon saw that by instinct she knew exactly what to do; she started at the inner part of the hind legs, where the skin is softest, then tore out the guts, and after enjoying these delicacies, buried the stomach contents and covered up the blood spoor, as all proper lions do. Then she gnawed the meat off the bones with her molars and rasped it away with her rough tongue.

Once we knew that she could do this it was time for us to let her do her own killing. The plain was covered with isolated bush clusters, ideal hide-outs for any animal. All the lions had to do, when they wanted a meal, was to wait under cover until an antelope approached downwind, rush out, and get their dinner.

We now left Elsa alone for two or three days at a time, hoping that hunger would make her kill. But when we came back we always found her waiting for us and hungry. It was heartbreaking having to stick to our program, when obviously all she wanted was to be with us and sure of our affection. This she showed very clearly by sucking my thumbs and holding on to us with her paws. All the same we knew that for her good we must persevere.

By now we realized that it was going to take us much longer to release her to nature than we had expected; we therefore asked the Government if we could use our long leave in the country for the purpose of carrying out this experiment, and, very kindly, they consented. After receiving this permission we felt much relieved since we knew that we should now have the time required for our task.

We increased the number of days on which Elsa was left on her own, and we reinforced the thorn fences round our tents so that they were strong enough to keep any lion out. This we did specifically to prevent Elsa from visiting us when she was hungry.

One morning, when she was with us, we located a lion who seemed placid and in a good mood; she stepped off the car and we tactfully left the pair alone. That evening while sitting in our thorn-protected tent we suddenly heard Elsa's miaow, and before we could stop her she crept through the thorns and settled down with us. She was bleeding from claw marks and had walked eight miles back, obviously preferring our company to that of the lion.

The next time we took her a longer distance away from camp.

As we drove we saw two eland bulls, each weighing about fifteen hundred pounds, engaged in a fight. Elsa promptly jumped off the car and stalked them. At first they were so absorbed in their fight that they did not notice her, but when they became aware of her presence she narrowly missed a savage kick from one of them. They broke off the fight and Elsa chased them a short distance and finally came back very proud of herself.

Soon afterward we met two young lions sitting on the grass in the open. They looked to us ideal companions for Elsa, but by now she was very suspicious of our tricks and would not leave the car, although she talked very agitatedly to them. As we had no means of dropping her off, we had to miss this opportunity and went on until we met two Thomson's gazelles fighting; this sight caused Elsa to jump off and we drove quickly away, leaving her to learn more about wild life.

It was nearly a week before we returned. We found her waiting, and very hungry. She was full of affection; we had deceived her so often, broken faith with her, done so much to destroy her trust in us, yet she remained loyal. We dropped some meat which we had brought with us, and she immediately started to eat it. Suddenly we heard unmistakable growls and soon saw two lions trotting fast toward us. They were obviously on the hunt and probably they had scented the meat; they approached very quickly. Poor Elsa took in the situation and bolted as hurriedly as she could, leaving her precious meal. At once a little jackal appeared that up till now must have been hiding in the grass; he lost no time in taking his chance and began to take bite after bite at Elsa's meat, knowing that his luck was not going to last long. This proved true, for one of the lions advanced steadily upon him, uttering threatening growls. But meat was meat and the little jackal was not to be easily frightened away; he held on to his possession and took as many bites as he could until the lion was practically on top of him. Even then, with unbelievable pluck he tried to save his meal. But size prevailed over courage and the lion was the winner. Elsa watched this scene from a distance and saw her first meal, after so many days, being taken away from her. In the circumstances it seemed hard that the two lions took no interest in anything but their food and completely ignored her. To compensate her for her disappointment we took her away.

While we were in camp we had some human visitors. Late one morning a Land Rover drove up to camp containing a Roman Catholic missionary and a well-known Kenya personality and his young son. They had come to look at game. George asked them in and was just

Elsa on the Land Rover

about to explain that we had a tame lioness in camp when Elsa, hearing the car, came bounding in, full of curiosity and friendliness. With her usual good manners she made for the visitors, to greet them. They looked a little startled, to say the least of it, particularly the holy father, but I must say they took it very well. Then Elsa, having done her duty, flung herself down beside the table and went to sleep.

Then a Swiss couple, having heard that we had a lion cub, came to see it. I think they had visions of something small which could be picked up and cuddled, but seeing the three-hundred-odd-pound Elsa on the roof of the Land Rover made them pause, and it was a little time before we could persuade them to get out of their car and join us at lunch. Elsa was courtesy itself, welcomed the strangers, and only once swept the table clear with her tail. After this, they could not have enough of her and had themselves photographed with her at every angle.

We had been in camp for four weeks, and although Elsa had spent most of the last fortnight in the bush she had not yet started killing for herself. By now the rains had begun and every afternoon there were heavy showers. The conditions in this region were very different to those at Isiolo. For one thing, it was much colder; for another, while the ground at Isiolo is sandy and dries within a few hours, here there was black cotton soil which turns into a morass after rain; moreover, it is covered with waist-high grass which prevents it from drying for weeks on end. At home Elsa had enjoyed the rains and had been invigorated by them, but here she was very miserable.

One night very heavy rain fell without stopping; at least five inches came down before daybreak and the country was flooded. In the morning we waded out often knee-deep in mud, and we met Elsa already halfway back to camp. She looked so unhappy and wanted so desperately to stay with us that we took her home. That evening we suddenly heard a terrified galloping come past our camp, followed by a stillness. What drama was happening outside? Next arose the hysterical chuckles of hyena mingled with the high-pitched yells of jackal, but these were soon silenced by the growls of at least three lions. We realized that they must have killed just outside the camp. What a chance for Elsa. But while we listened, fascinated, to the grandiose chorus of shrill, piercing, staccato noises interspersed with deep guttural rumblings, she rubbed her head against us and showed how glad she was to be inside the thorn fence in our company.

After a few days the rain decreased and we renewed our efforts to turn Elsa into a wild lioness. But she had become so suspicious of being deserted again that we had great difficulty in inducing her to follow us into the plains.

She did, however, in the end accompany us and we met two lionesses who came hurriedly toward the car, but Elsa bolted from them and seemed more nervous than ever.

It was evident that in this place she was scared of lions, so we decided not to go on trying to force her to make friends with them, but

Out!

to wait till she came into season again, then perhaps she would choose her own mate by mutual attraction.

Meanwhile we would concentrate our efforts on training her to kill her food and thus to become independent of us. Also, once she could kill, she would be a more suitable partner for a lion, should she decide to join one. The plains were still under water and most of the game had concentrated on the few bits of slightly higher ground which were drier. Elsa loved one little hillock which was studded with rocks, and we therefore chose this place as her experimental headquarters. It was unfortunately only eight miles from our camp; it would have been better if we could have moved off to a greater distance, but under the existing weather conditions this was not practicable.

We left Elsa for a week on her hillock, but when we returned she looked so unhappy that it needed all my will power to harden myself sufficiently to carry on with her education. We sat with her during the midday lull until she dozed off with her head on my lap. Suddenly, in the bush, just behind us, there was a frightening crash and a rhino appeared. We both jumped up like lightning, and while I ran behind a tree, Elsa gallantly charged the intruder and drove it away. Most unfairly, during her absence we deserted her again.

Late that afternoon the atmosphere became heavy with moisture, and the setting sun was spectacularly reflected against dark red curtains of cloud hanging out of a gray sky pierced by fragments of parallel rainbows. This kaleidoscope of luminous color changed rapidly into threatening dark clouds loaded with rain which finally towered above us in one black mass. All was in suspense waiting for the firmament to burst.

Then a few heavy drops fell like lead to the ground, and now, as if two giant hands had torn the heavens apart, a deluge descended with such torrential force that soon our camp was in the middle of a running stream. For hours the flood continued. I imagined poor Elsa alone in this icy night, drenched, shivering, and miserable; thunder and lightning added to my nightmare. Next morning we waded the eight miles to

138

Elsa's siesta

the ridge where we had left her. As usual, she was waiting for us, over-joyed to see us, and greeted us each in turn by rubbing her head and body against us repeatedly, uttering her moaning noise. But today there was no doubt that she was miserable; indeed, she was nearly cry-ing. We decided that, though it would interrupt her education, we could not leave her out in such weather. Unlike the local lions used to this climate, she came from semidesert country and could not quickly adapt herself to very different conditions. Now she was pleased to walk back with us splashing in her familiar Isiolo way through the swamp and showing how happy she was.

Next day she was ill. When she moved she was in great pain; her glands were swollen and she had a temperature. We made her a bed of grass in the annex to George's tent, and there she lay, panting, listless, and pathetic. I treated her with M and B, the only drug which I thought might help. She wanted me to be near her all the time, which, of course, I was.

The rains had now set in; even a car with a four-wheel drive could not plow through to the nearest place at which blood slides could be tested, so we sent a runner the hundred-odd miles with various sam-ples. The reply, when it came, stated that Elsa was infected with hook-worm and tapeworm, from both of which she had previously suffered and which we knew how to treat. But neither of these troubles could account for her swollen glands or her temperature. We believed that she had also become infected by some tick-borne virus. If this proved true it would suggest that an animal, immune to diseases in its own environment, when transferred to another does not carry the same immunity to local strains, and might be one explanation for the often puzzling distribution of animals found in East Africa.

Elsa became so ill that for a time we did not think that she would recover. However, after a week the fever became intermittent; every three or four days her temperature would rise and then go back again to normal. She was rapidly losing her beautiful golden color, her coat was dull, like cotton wool, and she developed many white hairs on her back. Her face became ash gray. She had difficulty in dragging herself from the tent into the sparse sunshine; the only hopeful sign was her appetite. We gave her as much meat and milk as she wanted, although both had to be fetched from a long distance. We also succeeded in spite of the transport difficulties arising from the weather in corresponding regularly with the Veterinary Laboratory in Nairobi, but as no sign of a parasite was found in the samples we provided we had to treat her more or less by guesswork.

We dosed her for hookworm and for Rickettsia, a tick-borne parasite, which had been suggested as a possible cause of her illness, but as it was impossible to insert a hypodermic needle into a gland in order to obtain the fluid from which her illness might have been diagnosed, all we could do was to keep her as quiet as possible and give her the affection she needed. She was very gentle and responsive to all we did for her and often hugged me with her paws when I rested my head on her shoulders.

During her illness, because she lived so intimately with us, Elsa became more dependent on us and tamer than ever. Most of the day

Elsa and the author

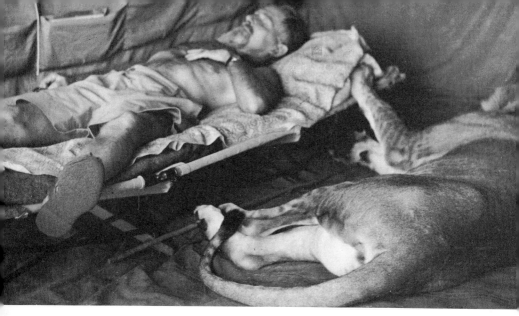

Elsa usually slept beside George

she lay across the entrance to our thorn-fence enclosure, in a strategic position, which enabled her to watch all that went on inside the camp and outside on the plain as well. At mealtimes she preferred to have the boys step over her as they brought in our food than to move from her place. The staff laughingly competed at running the gauntlet while balancing full soup plates, getting spanked by Elsa in a friendly way as they passed over her.

She slept in the tent with George but was free to come and go as she pleased. Late one night he was awakened by her low calls and heard her trying to get out of the back of the tent. He sat up and saw a shape in the doorway of the tent. Thinking that Elsa could not have got around so quickly, he switched on his torch and saw a wild lioness blinking in the glare. He shouted at her and she went off. No doubt she had scented Elsa and, reassured by the lion noises coming from inside the tent, had decided to investigate.

It was now five weeks since Elsa's illness had started, and her condition had improved only slightly. It was plain that the climate in this region was against her, also that she might not be immune from local infections such as ticks and tsetse, which vary according to localities. Besides this, she was different in appearance from the local lions— much darker in color, with a longer nose, bigger ears, and generally much smaller. In every way she belonged to the semidesert and not to the highlands. Finally, being in a game reserve meant that not only did George have to go twenty miles by car to get outside the reserve to shoot meat for her, but also that he could not take her hunting with him and thereby give her the opportunity of being in at the kill and getting the feel of pulling down a live animal—an experience which, in her wild state, she would have gained from her mother. It was evident therefore that after having camped here for three months we must try to choose a better home for her.

It was not easy to find an area which had a suitable climate, permanent water, enough game to supply her with food, and no tribesmen or hunting parties; moreover, it needed to be accessible by car. Eventually

Elsa affectionate as ever

we discovered such a paradise and received the Government's permission to release a lion there. As soon as the rains ceased we decided to go there.

Camp was struck, and everything loaded into the cars—everything except Elsa. She chose that very day to come into season and had disappeared into the bush. We had waited for two and a half months for just this to happen, but we knew now that we could not allow her to go wild in this area. During the day there was no sign of her. We hunted for her everywhere, in the Land Rover and on foot, but without success; finally we became very worried in case she might have been killed by a wild lioness. However, there was nothing to do but wait for her return. For two days and nights she kept away, except for one short visit during which she rushed up to us, rubbed her head against our knees, and dashed off again, only to come back a few minutes later, indulge in some more rubbings, then make off a second time and as quickly return, as though to tell us: "I am very happy, but please understand I *must* go. I just came to tell you not to worry." Then she was off again.[1] When she finally returned, for good, she was badly scratched and bleeding from several claw marks and was very irritable when I tried to dress her wounds. It needed much patience to make her jump into the truck.

Thus ended the first three months of our experiment. We had failed this time owing to her illness but felt confident that given time and patience we would succeed.

[1] We often wondered why Elsa never produced cubs as a result of being with a lion while she was in season. Later I learned from a zoo authority that during the four relevant days the male sires the female at least six to eight times a day and that it is thought that it is only on the fourth day that the siring becomes effective. If this is so, it is obvious that Elsa never had sufficient opportunity as the jealous lioness, holding guard over her male, would not be likely to tolerate too frequent love-making with a newcomer to the pride.

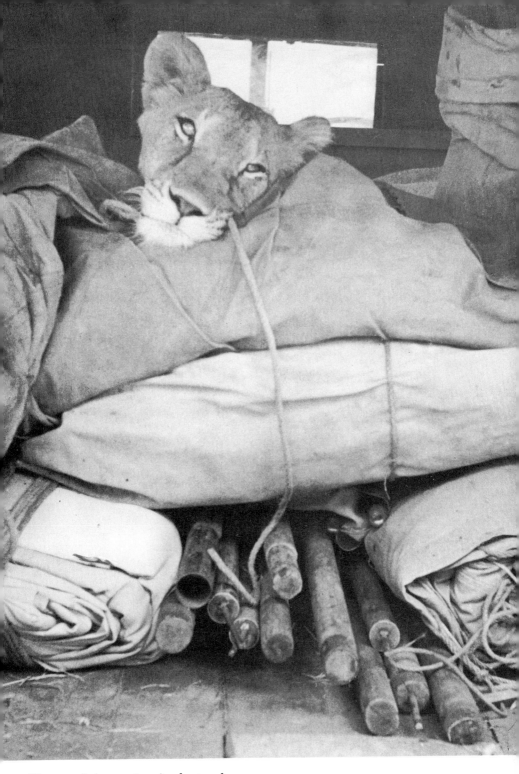

Elsa travels in comfort in the truck

The Second Release

N o w we had before us a journey of about four hundred and forty miles. On some trips everything seems to go wrong, and this was one of them. After only twelve miles, one of the front bearings went on George's car. I drove to the nearest Administrative Post, which was ninety miles away, to get a new one sent out. I had to spend the night there with poor Elsa locked up in the back of my car. Meanwhile, when the bearing reached George he found that he had no spanner large enough to fit, but by using a hammer and a cold chisel he finally managed to get it fixed by the evening, and joined me. During that night and the following morning we had six punctures; finally at nine in the evening, when we were still twelve miles short of our destination, my car began to make the most alarming noise. So we stopped and put up our camp beds in the open. We were all completely exhausted after fifty-two hours of continuous driving. Elsa had behaved splendidly and had never made a protest; now she just flung herself down beside us and went to sleep. Next morning we thought that we might have great difficulty in persuading her to re-enter the car, particularly as she had already gone off to lie up for the day in the dense reeds growing by a little stream near our camp. Crossing the stream was going to be difficult, so we decided to get the cars across first, and then collect Elsa.

The Land Rover went through without trouble, but my car got stuck and had to be towed out. We then recrossed the stream on foot to try to persuade Elsa to leave her shady retreat and follow us back to the cars. She came at once and jumped in my car, as though she knew that

Elsa at her new home

the journey was not yet at an end and wished to co-operate. We started off along a rough track through thick bush which George had cut during the Mau Mau rebellion, when it had been thought that this remote corner might become a convenient hide-out for Mau Mau gangs. Even now our troubles were not over; a few miles farther on a rear spring in my car broke, so it was late in the afternoon when we reached Elsa's new home.

It was truly a corner of Africa where "the foxes say good night to each other." To reach an ideal camp site, George and the boys cut a new track, through thick bush; it took them four days. Our final camp was on a beautiful river lined by walls of doum palms, acacias, and fig trees interwoven with creepers. The water rushed foaming and bubbling through rapids, passed between islands covered with reeds and in the farther reaches calmed into many rock-bound pools of cool clear water, deep enough to hold many fish. It was a fisherman's paradise, and George could not wait to get out his rod.

The country was quite different from the region we had left. It was much hotter; there were no great herds of game grazing peacefully on grassy plains; only thornbush, with visibility reduced to a few yards—a hunter's nightmare. But it was only thirty-five miles from Elsa's birthplace and was the type of country that was natural to her.

When we left the lush tropical greenery, which was confined to the riverbanks, we felt the intense heat of the sun hitting us like a hot wave. We were within a short distance of the equator; our altimeter read sixteen hundred feet. The dense dry thornbush was penetrable only by a network of game paths; these were also useful in warning us of elephant, rhino, and buffalo whose spoor and droppings left no doubt that the paths were in daily use. About two hundred yards from the camp there was a salt lick, and many impressions of rhino horns and elephant tusks in the salt told us that they were frequent visitors to it; also nearly every tree of any size had its bark polished or worn off by elephants rubbing their bodies against it. Because of this Elsa found it difficult to do her daily claw exercises, as there were few trees left with any rough bark. Only the baobabs; their giant purple-gray shapes towering over the low thornbush were untouched, for their smooth trunks were of no use to animals.

The great attraction of the place was a huge ridge of reddish rock with cliffs and caves, in whose shadows we saw hyrax dashing about. It was an ideal lion's home, with a splendid lookout. From its top we watched giraffe, waterbuck, lesser kudu, gerenuk, and bushbuck moving toward the river which was their life artery in this otherwise waterless semidesert country.

Either as a result of our Rickettsia treatment or owing to the change in climate, Elsa's condition improved daily, so we were able to restart her education. Every morning, as soon as it got light, we took

148

Hollow baobab trees attracted Elsa

Elsa watches out for game from her rock

Elsa for a walk, and did so again in the afternoon. These walks, which took us along the numerous game paths and sandy watercourses, were full of interest. Elsa loved them; she sniffed and followed the spoor of animals which had been there during the previous night, rolled in elephant and rhino droppings, and chased wart hogs and dik-diks. We, too, were on the alert, taking note of animal tracks, their freshness and direction, which way the wind was blowing, and kept ears and eyes open for telltale sounds and sights. This was necessary because otherwise one was apt to run unexpectedly into rhino, buffalo, or elephant, and it is these surprise meetings at close quarters which can lead to trouble.

Here, unlike the first place to which we had taken her, Elsa was able to go out hunting with George. We both hate killing animals, but now we had to make some sacrifices to Elsa's education, and the knowledge that in her natural state she would have been killing them on her own account appeased our qualms. The sooner she learned to do it properly, the better for all concerned. For the present she must stalk her quarry, then, if she were not able to kill, George would

Every morning we took Elsa for a walk

bring the animal down with a bullet and leave her to give the *coup de grâce*. After this she would be left to protect her kill against vultures, hyenas, and lions, and in this way would meet these animals in natural circumstances.

We heard several lions close to the camp and often saw their pug-marks.

One evening Elsa did not come back from her favorite lookout on top of the rocks. It was a splendid place where she found the breeze cool, where no tsetse fly molested her, and from which she could watch the animals below. But as we had only been a short time in the area, we were worried at her absence and went out to look for her. By then it was well after dark, the bush was alive with dangerous animals, and we found creeping through the dense scrub nerve-racking. There was no sign of Elsa, so, defeated, we returned.

At dawn we resumed our search, and soon found her pugmarks mixed up with those of a large lion; the spoors led down to the river and reappeared on the far side. Here there were outcrops of rock, and we thought that perhaps the lion had his domain there and had taken Elsa to his lie-up.

About lunchtime a wild chatter started up among the baboons near the camp; we hoped that this might herald Elsa's return and, sure enough, soon she came, swimming across the river. She greeted us, rubbing her head against us in turn and talking to us excitedly about her adventure. We were glad not to find any scratches on her. Since it was only a fortnight since she had been badly treated by a lion when we were still at our former camp, we hoped that the fact that her new escapade had been voluntary was a good augury for her release.

One morning a waterbuck offered an excellent opportunity for initiating Elsa into killing. George shot it, but before it fell Elsa jumped at its throat and hung on like a bulldog until in a few minutes the animal died of suffocation. It was her first experience of killing a large animal of about her own weight. We now saw that she knew the vital spot by instinct and also the way of effecting a quick death;

in fact, she had made use of a lion's normal method of killing a prey, which is not as some people imagine by breaking its neck. She first ate the tail, and this, as we were to discover, became her normal practice; then she opened the animal between the hind legs, ate the guts, and carefully buried the stomach, covering up all traces of blood. Might this be a way of deceiving the vultures? Then she seized the buck by the neck and, straddling it between her forepaws, dragged it into a strategically well-chosen spot, in this case a shady thicket some fifty yards away. We left her there to guard her kill by day from vultures and, after dark, from hyenas. One frequently hears stories of lions carrying their victims away by swinging them across their backs. Neither George nor I have ever seen a lion act in this way, though it is true that they will carry a small animal such as a dog or a hare in their mouths. We have always seen them drag anything larger in the way which Elsa used on this and all other occasions.

About teatime we went back to visit her, and took her water. Although she loved her afternoon walk with us, this time she made no attempt to leave her kill. When it became dark she did not return, but

Elsa enjoyed the river, especially on a hot day

about three in the morning we were awakened by a heavy cloudburst and soon after this she appeared and spent the rest of the night in camp.

Early in the morning we all went out to see what had happened to her kill. Of course it had disappeared, and the ground was patterned with lion and hyena spoor. Near by, we heard some lion grunts; these made us wonder whether it was the rain or the lions which had made Elsa leave her kill during the night.

Although Elsa's health had greatly improved, she was still far from her usual self and preferred to spend most of her day in camp. In order to break this habit and to make her lie up in the cool shade of the river, George took her out fishing with him. She would watch intently for the slightest ripple in the water, and as soon as he hooked a fish she plunged into the river to give the wriggling creature the *coup de grâce* and retrieve it. Sometimes we had great difficulty in removing the hook before she dashed off to camp with the fish; once there, she usually placed the fish on George's bed, as if to say: "This cold, strange kill is yours," and then she would return to await the next catch. This new

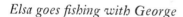

Elsa goes fishing with George

game was great fun, but we needed to find another device to attract her away from the camp.

Close to the river stood a magnificent tree, its branches nearly sweeping the water. Under its green canopy, protected by its cool shade and subdued light from the glaring sun, I felt as though I were under a dome. Here, concealed by the low branches, I watched many wild creatures, lesser kudu and bushbuck, which came to the river to drink; a hammer-headed stork also came to quench his thirst, and there were baboons; they provided the real fun. Sitting there with Elsa close to me, I felt as though I were on the doorstep of paradise: man and beast in trusting harmony; the slow-flowing river adding to the idyll. I thought that this place would make a stimulating "studio" for me to paint or write in, so we nailed some boards across a wooden frame and improvised a table and bench, and soon I began to work there, leaning against the broad trunk of the tree.

Standing on her hind legs, Elsa inspected my paintbox and typewriter suspiciously; and resting both her front paws on the unfortunate

In the studio

tools, she licked my face and wanted to be assured of my affection before I was allowed to start work. Then she settled down at my feet and I began, full of inspiration; but I had not reckoned with our audience. As soon as I tried to concentrate I heard the inquiring bark of a baboon peeping through the foliage; then the bush on the opposite bank became alive with inquisitive watching faces. Soon, intrigued by Elsa, they came more and more into the open, swinging recklessly from tree to tree, screaming and barking, sliding backwards down the trunks or hopping and swaying like shadows in the treetops, until one little chap fell with a splash into the river. At once an old baboon came to its rescue and, clutching the wet, struggling creature, raced off with it to safety. At this, all the baboons in the world seemed to have got loose and the screeching was deafening. Elsa, who could tolerate the noise no longer, plunged into the river and swam across, accompanied by the hilarious shrieks of the baboons. As soon as she had reached firm ground she jumped at the nearest of the little tormentors. He swung

156

Elsa still sucked my thumb when nervous

tantalizingly low but nimbly avoided a spanking by hopping to a higher branch, from which place of safety he pulled faces and shook the branch at Elsa. The others joined in the game, and the more infuriated Elsa became the more they enjoyed teasing her—they sat just out of her reach, scratching their posteriors, pretending to be utterly unaware of the raging lioness just below. The scene was so funny that in spite of Elsa's humiliation I opened my camera and filmed it. This was too much for her; as soon as she saw me focusing the hated box on her she splashed back through the river, and before I had time to secure the camera she leapt on me and we both rolled over in the sand with the precious Bolex. Everything was wet; the baboons applauded our performance enthusiastically, and I fear that in the eyes of our audience both Elsa and I lost face very considerably.

After this the baboons looked every day for Elsa, and both sides got to know each other very well. As she tolerated their provocations and took to ignoring them, they grew bolder and bolder. Often they squatted for their daily drinks at the edge of the rapids, separated from her by only a few yards of water. One would keep sentry duty while the others sat on their haunches and, bending low, slowly drank their fill.

They were not the only cheeky small animals who annoyed Elsa. For instance, once when we had brought back a buck a monitor lizard appeared. These harmless large lizards, which are about three to five feet long and four to six inches wide, have forked tongues, they live in rivers and eat fish, but also enjoy meat. A superstition is that they give warning of the approach of crocodiles; in fact, they do eat the eggs of crocodiles and so act as one of nature's controls. Now, this one endeavored to snatch a few bites from Elsa's meal. She tried to catch him, but he was much too quick for her. So she covered the kill safely out of his reach, and thus prevented him from stealing another scrap of her carcass. This behavior was in contrast to her attitude toward us. She liked me to hold her food for her while she ate it and would allow George and Nuru to handle her "kill." We were her "pride" and she was quite prepared to share everything with us, but she had no intention of sharing with a monitor. In fact, she also differentiated between myself, George, Nuru, and the rest of our staff; she would, for instance, allow any of us to take her meat out of the tent, but she did not allow the boys or the cook to do so.

Our idyll would have been perfect if Elsa had not been a carnivore which had to be trained to kill. Our next victim was a gerenuk. After Elsa had done her share in the killing we left her, some miles away from our camp, in charge of the carcass. On our way home we saw a lion walking in her direction. Had he already scented the kill? When, in the afternoon, we went to visit Elsa, she as well as the kill had gone, but plenty of big lion spoor told us what had happened. We followed her pugmarks for over two miles; they led toward her favorite rock, on which, with our field glasses, we eventually detected her. She had been clever enough to choose the only spot where she felt strategically safe from lions and could also be seen by us from a distance.

One night we were awakened by snorts and commotions coming from the direction of the salt lick. Before we were properly awake, Elsa rushed out of the tent to protect her "den." There followed more snorts and commotions, which gradually faded away. Evidently Elsa had done her stuff; soon she returned panting, flung herself down next to George's bed, and, putting one paw on him, seemed to say: "Now all is safe again. It was only a rhino."

She did the same thing a few nights later with a herd of elephants. Their startled screams coming from behind the camp were enough to send her into action, and fortunately she succeeded in chasing the giants away. Their trumpeting was terrifying. I am always scared of elephants—they are the only big game which really do frighten me. Now I could not help thinking how easily the situation might have been reversed. The elephants might have chased Elsa, and she would of course have come back to us for protection. George laughed at my fears, but I felt far from confident in always trusting to luck.

Every day a buffalo approached our camp until one morning he became a victim: George shot him. Although he was dead long before Elsa arrived, she went wild with excitement—indeed, she got far more worked up over this carcass than we had ever seen her before at a kill. She pounced madly on the dead buffalo, attacking from every side and turning somersaults across the body. But however uncontrolled her movements seemed to be, she took good care to keep out of reach of the deadly horns. Finally she tapped the buffalo on the nose with her paw to make sure that he was dead.

Elsa learns to open a buffalo

George's main purpose in shooting such a big beast had been to attract wild lions to the kill. We hoped that if they came, Elsa could join in the feast and make friends with them. In order to control whatever might happen, we decided to drag the carcass close to the camp and then leave Elsa in charge of it. Meanwhile we went off to fetch the car. When we returned the trees around were weighed down with vultures and marabou storks, but Elsa was keeping them at bay, sitting out in the hot sun next to her kill. She was plainly much relieved when we, her "pride," took over and made it possible for her to retire to a shady bush. But as soon as the boys started to cut open the inch-thick skin of the buffalo, she could not resist it and rushed up to join in. While they were slicing open the stomach, she helped, tore out guts between the busy knives, and chewed them with delight under the very hands of the butchering boys. She sucked the intestines into her mouth like spaghetti, at the same time pressing with her teeth so that the unwanted contents were ejected like toothpaste from a tube. Good-naturedly she watched the carcass being fastened to a chain and attached to the car. Then while the poor Land Rover jerked across uneven ground towing the heavy buffalo, she rode—as usual—on the canvas roof, adding another three hundred pounds to the load.

After the kill had been secured with a chain to a tree close to camp, Elsa guarded it jealously during the whole of the following day and night. Judging by the never-ending chorus of high-pitched chuckles from hyenas, she was kept very busy after dark, but next morning when we returned she was still protecting the carcass. Only then did she leave it, making it very plain that it was now *our* turn to be on guard while she trotted away to the river. We covered the kill with thorns as a protection from vultures and so saved it for another night's "defense" lesson.

Elsa joined us on our usual afternoon's walk, her swaying belly full of buffalo meat. After a short time through the bush she spotted a hyena making its way slowly toward the kill. Immediately she froze, her left front paw suspended in the air. Then, with the utmost caution, she lowered herself to a crouching position, blending among the straw-colored grass till she was almost invisible. Tense with controlled excitement, she watched the hyena hobbling peacefully along, quite unaware that it had an audience. When it came to within a few yards Elsa rushed forward and gave it a well-aimed smack. With a yell the animal rolled over and lay on its back emitting howls and long-drawn moans. Elsa looked at us and jerked her head in her characteristic way toward her victim, as though saying: "What shall we do next?" As she did not get any encouragement from us, she started licking her paws and appeared utterly bored by the miserable creature in front of her. Gradually the

hyena pulled itself together and eventually, still whining protests, sneaked away.

Elsa's trust in us was shown on other occasions.

Late one afternoon we had left her in charge of a buck which she and George had killed a long distance from the camp. Knowing that she would not remain with it alone during the night so far away from us, we collected a car to bring it nearer to camp. But on our return, Elsa and the kill had gone. Soon, however, she appeared through the bush and led us to the hide-out to which she had dragged it during our absence. Although she was very pleased to see us, she would not allow us to pull the kill to the car, and all the tricks I tried to make her leave it failed: she was not going to be fooled. Finally we maneuvered the car in front of the carcass, and I pointed first to the car and then to the buck, then to the car and again to the buck, trying to make her see that we wanted to help her. She must have understood, for suddenly she got up, rubbed her head against my knees, and pulled her kill from under the thornbush toward the car. Finally she tried to lift it by the head into the Land Rover; soon realizing that she could not do this from outside, she then leapt into the car, and from there, gripping the head, pulled with all her strength while we lifted the hindquarters. When the buck was safely inside, Elsa sat on it panting, while George drove on. However, she found that bumping through the bush was not at all comfortable in her cramped position, so she jumped out again and onto the roof, bending her head frequently to see if all was well inside and the kill still there.

When we arrived at the camp we had to face the problem of getting the buck out of the car, but now Elsa treated us as her allies and let us do most of the pulling. Everyone was helping except myself, so Elsa walked up to me and gave me an encouraging spank, as though to say: "What about your helping too?"

Although we had left the kill fairly near the camp, we soon heard her dragging it along with the intention, no doubt, of bringing it inside our tent. We quickly closed the thorn fence, locking her out with her smelly buck. Poor Elsa, it was much safer inside the tent; now she would have to spend the whole night protecting it. The best thing she could do was to place it against the outside of the thorn fence, and this she did. As a result, the hyenas came so close and made so much noise that sleep was impossible. Finally Elsa must have got tired of chasing the creatures away, for we heard her dragging the buck toward the river and then splashing through the water with it. This defeated the hyenas and they left. Did she know that they would not follow her through water?

Next morning we found her spoor and the marks left by dragging the kill. They led across the river, but then, it seemed, she had not wanted to be separated from us and so she had dragged it back to our side. Here she had placed it in impenetrable bush, right at the water's

Elsa helps to get the buck out of the Land Rover

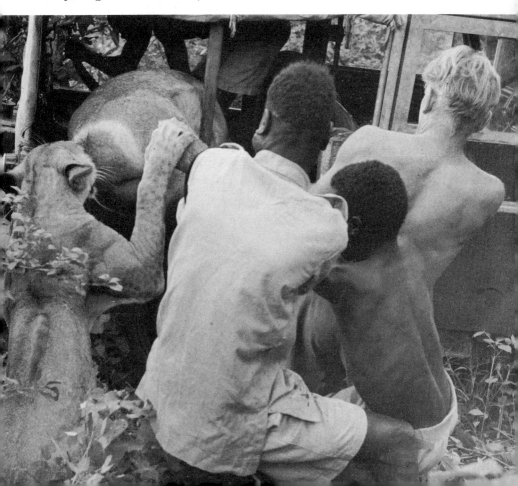

edge, so that no animal could get at it unless they approached from the river. We now found her resting with the buck, and she made it obvious that she was very much hurt that we had locked her out; it took us a long time to win back her confidence and to be forgiven.

Although Elsa had no mother to teach her, she knew by instinct how far she could go with wild animals. Many times on our walks through the bush we watched her, sniffing the air and then stalking determinedly in one direction until we heard the crashing of big bodies breaking through the woods. On several occasions she detected rhinos and chased them away from us; in fact, she was an excellent watchdog.

Several herds of buffalo had made their home on a near-by ridge and Elsa never missed an opportunity of stirring these heavy animals into commotion. More than once she surprised them fast asleep, dodged around them, hopping nimbly out of range of their horns, and she always stood her ground until the buffaloes departed.

One morning we walked in a dry river bed and read the "news" about last night's visitors in the sand. Two lions and plenty of elephants were of major importance. The sun was getting hot and we were all tired after a three hours' walk. The wind was against us and, coming carelessly around a bend, we nearly collided with a herd of elephants. Luckily, Elsa was trotting a short distance behind us, so we had time to jump onto the high bank, while the elephants climbed up the other side and took three tiny calves into safety, and one old bull kept in the rear, ready to charge should there be any nonsense. Elsa came sleepily along, then, seeing the bull, sat down. We watched, wondering what would happen. Both sides looked at each other for what seemed to us an endless time. Finally, it was the elephant who gave in and joined his herd, while Elsa rolled on her back, getting rid of some tsetse flies.

On our way home George shot a waterbuck which was standing in the river. Badly hit, it dashed across to the opposite side, followed by Elsa, who splashed unbelievably fast through the deep water. When we arrived at the other bank we found her among the river bush, panting, on top of the dead buck. She was very excited and did not

Makedde and Elsa

allow us to touch her kill. So we decided to return home and leave her to guard it. As soon as we started wading back through the water, she began to follow us, but seemed torn between conflicting impulses: she did not want to be left on the wrong side of the river with her kill, and on the other hand she did not want to lose it. Eventually she returned reluctantly to it, but soon made another attempt to cross, only to turn back again but undecidedly. However, by the time we had reached the opposite bank Elsa had made up her mind.

Now we saw her dragging the buck into the water. What was she up to? Surely she could not bring this heavy animal across alone? But Elsa was not going to be defeated. She held the carcass in her mouth and swam with it through the deep water, her head often submerged to get a better grip. She hauled and tugged, pushed and pulled, and when the buck got stuck, pounced on it to get it floating again. Often both disappeared from view and only Elsa's tail or one leg of the buck told us of the struggle that was going on at the bottom of the river. We watched fascinated. After half an hour of strenuous effort, she trailed her quarry proudly through the shallow water near to us. By now she was really exhausted, but her task was not finished yet. After tugging the buck into a little sheltered bay where the current could not carry it away, she looked for a safe hiding place. The bank here was a solid network of sharp-edged, thorn-hooked doum palm seedlings, which overhung the steep walls that lined the river; even Elsa could not penetrate this thicket.

We left her with her kill and went back to camp to collect some bush knives and ropes and to have our overdue breakfast. When we returned we cut a passage through the doum palm undergrowth to the water's edge, and while Elsa watched the men suspiciously I slipped a rope noose over the buck's head. Now all was ready to haul it up the steep bank. At the first tug Elsa growled and flattened her ears warningly—obviously she thought that her kill was going to be taken away from her. But as soon as she saw me join in the pulling, she relaxed and climbed up the bank. Our combined efforts landed the buck ten feet above the river, where the boys had cut a well-protected shady shelter for Elsa and her kill. Now she realized what we had done for her, and it was touching to see her going from one to another of us, rubbing her head and thanking everyone in turn with a low moan.

On two occasions I watched her walk unconcernedly through a broad stream of black soldier ants, scattering their organized columns in all directions with her large paws. Although these fierce ants usually bite at anything which disturbs their migration, for some reason they did not take their revenge on Elsa.

One day we were very tired and I was walking along absent-mindedly behind Elsa. Suddenly she gave a terrific grunt, reared up on her hind legs, and leapt back. We were passing a tree which forked about five feet above the ground, and now coiled up in it I saw a red cobra erecting its hood toward us. Thanks to Elsa, nothing happened, but to pass a cobra at such close range might have been serious. It was the first time I had seen one in a tree. Even Elsa was impressed, and during the next few days she made a careful detour whenever we came near to that tree.

At this time it was very hot and Elsa spent much of her time in the river. Often she stood half submerged in the cool water; although we often saw crocodiles, they never seemed to worry her. Whenever George shot a guinea fowl near the river, Elsa retrieved it from the water and used its rescue as an excuse for prolonged splashings with the bird in her mouth; she enjoyed the game just as much as we loved watching her.

She had now completely recovered and was perfectly fit. She was very conservative in her habits, and except for slight variations our routine was the same every day: an early morning walk, followed by her midday slumber close to me by our tree on the riverbank. This lasted until teatime, then came our afternoon stroll. On our return she found her meal waiting for her; she usually carried it onto the roof

Elsa and prey in the river

of the Land Rover, where she remained until the lights were put out and everybody went to bed. Then she joined George in his tent, sleeping next to his bed on the ground, a paw always in touch with him.

One afternoon Elsa refused to come for a walk. When we returned after dark she had disappeared and did not return until early next morning. Later we found large lion pugmarks close to camp, and when she came back I again noticed the peculiar smell which was typical of her being in season. Her manners were another indication of this condition. Although she was very friendly, the real affection was missing. Soon after breakfast she was off again and kept away all day. After dark we heard her hopping onto the Land Rover, and I went out at once to play with her. But she was aloof and very restless; jumped down, and vanished into the dark. During the night I heard her splashing in the river, to the accompaniment of agitated noises coming from alarmed baboons; this lasted until early morning. Then Elsa returned for a quick visit to the camp, tolerated George's pattings,

A long drink on a hot day

purred at him, and went off again. It was obvious that she was in love.

We knew now by experience that this period lasted about four days. Unlike the conditions in our former camp, everything here was favorable to giving her an opportunity to go back to her natural life. The right moment seemed to have come, so we decided to withdraw tactfully for one week and leave her alone—we hoped in the company of a mate. We had to act quickly in order to avoid her seeing our departure.

While we were packing, Elsa returned. We therefore arranged that while I looked after her George would break camp, drive the loaded cars a distance of about one mile, and send a message to me to join him when everything was ready.

I took Elsa away from the camp to our tree. Would this be the last time we should see it together? She knew something was wrong; and though I tried to keep to our normal routine and had taken the typewriter along and made the familiar tickings to appease her suspicions, she was not reassured, nor could I type properly for my mind was too upset. Although we had prepared ourselves for this release and hoped it might give Elsa a happier future than she would have living in captivity, it was a different matter when it came to making the break, and actually to cut through our affection and leave her, possibly never to see her again. Elsa must have felt my emotion for she rubbed her silky head against me.

The river flowed slowly in front of us, as it had flowed yesterday and it would flow tomorrow. A hornbill called, some dry leaves fell off the tree and were carried away by the water. Elsa was part of this life. She belonged to nature and not to man. We were "man" and we loved her and she had been brought up to love us. Would she be able to forget all that had been familiar to her until this morning? Would she go and hunt when she was hungry? Or would she wait trustfully for our return, knowing that up to now we had never let her down? I had just given her a kiss to reassure her of my affection and to give her a feeling of security, but was it a kiss of betrayal? How could she

Elsa and the author

know that it needed all the strength of my love for her to leave her now and give her back to nature—to let her learn to live alone until she might find her pride—her real pride?

Nuru came and called me away. He had brought some meat along, and Elsa followed him trustfully into the reeds and started to eat—then we stole away.

The Final Test

W E drove ten miles to another river, smaller but much deeper than the one we had left; here we intended to spend a week. Late in the afternoon George and I strolled along the bank; we walked quietly, our thoughts with Elsa. I realized acutely how much I had become dependent on her; how much I had for nearly three years lived the life of a lioness, shared her feelings, interests, and reactions. We had lived so intimately together that being alone seemed unbearable. I felt desperately lonely with no Elsa walking at my side, rubbing her head against me and letting me feel her soft skin and warm body. There was of course the hope of seeing her again in one week's time. How much that meant to me.

Suddenly George stopped, pointing ahead, and we sank to the ground. A lesser kudu advanced toward us, nibbling gracefully at the young buds of the undergrowth. Then it stopped grazing, lifted its head, and looked cautiously around, instinctively alert to every moving shadow or snapping twig. Although we were well hidden and on the right side of the wind, I wondered whether it had not sensed our presence? Or perhaps it was the natural inborn fear of danger which kept this beautiful animal so constantly on its guard? Its perfect proportions, its exquisite body markings and white stripes and the magnificently shaped horns make this antelope one of nature's masterpieces. We watched the kudu with intense pleasure while it browsed slowly from bush to bush till it eventually disappeared.

Next we heard a noise by the river and advancing carefully saw a hippo cow and her calf feeding in the lush vegetation on the opposite bank. The sun was still too hot for them to leave the cool water, so they remained comfortably half submerged while noiselessly crunching their dinner. We judged that, given the depth of the river, they must be standing on their hind legs as they plodded slowly sideways along the bank to the juicy leaves which hung over the water.

We watched this peaceful scene, but my heart was with Elsa. Then I noticed an elephant on the far bank, separated from us by only a few yards of water. He was the leader of a small herd which now approached the rapids opposite us as silently as ghosts. The gap in the rock bank was narrow and each elephant had to drink in turn, touching the water repeatedly with its trunk before it sucked it up in long draughts. When it had had its fill, each elephant carefully stepped back to make way for the next thirsty animal. . . . Meanwhile the herd huddled close together around two tiny calves, protecting them by their solid bodies from any danger that might lurk beyond.

The sun was sinking, and its warm light was reflected on the shiny fronds of the doum palms, tinting their tops with a golden glow.

Again I thought of Elsa—what a beautiful world she had been born into. Whatever losing her might mean to me, we must now try our utmost to give her back to this life and save her from a captive existence, in which she would be deprived of all that nature intended for her. Although up to now there was no record of a hand-reared lion being successfully liberated, we still hoped that Elsa would be able to adapt herself to wild life, to a life to which she had always been so close.

At last the week of anxiety ended and we went back to see how Elsa had stood up to the test.

When we arrived at our former camp we looked at once for her pugmarks; there was no sign of them. I began to call. Soon afterward we heard her familiar "hnk-hnk" and saw her coming from the river trotting as fast as she could. Her welcome showed us that she had

173

missed us as much as we had missed her and her rubbings and miaow-ings touched us deeply. We had brought her a buck, but she hardly glanced at it and continued her greetings. As soon as the great rejoic-ings were over I looked at her stomach: it was full. She must have eaten recently; this took a great load off my mind for it meant that she was now safe. She had proved that she could fend for herself and be independent of us, at least so far as food was concerned.

While our tents were being pitched I took her to the river and there we rested together. I was happy now and could relax, feeling that Elsa's future was assured. She must have felt the same, for she laid her big soft paw on me and dozed off. I was awakened by her raising her head and looking at a bushbuck, whose reddish shape appeared through the foliage on the opposite bank. Elsa watched with-out interest while the antelope stepped slowly along, unaware of our presence. However happy Elsa might be at the moment, I knew that her lack of interest in the buck was partly due to her full belly. What had she eaten? Some little vervet monkeys were watching us silently through the trees, but where were our noisy friends, the usually ever present baboons? Later on my fears about her first kill were confirmed, for we found tufts of baboon hair close to the drinking place, where they had so often teased Elsa.

Now that our minds were at ease regarding Elsa's future, we decided to enjoy her company for another short period and wait till an oppor-tunity occurred of making the final break, in some way which would not be too painful. We took up our life where we had left it off. Although Elsa seldom let us out of her sight, we thought it a good omen that she continued to follow her hunting instinct and sometimes when we were on our walks, deserted us for an hour.

The country had become very dry and often the sky was lit up by grass fires. The short rains were due in the next two or three weeks, and the parched ground was thirsty for their life-giving food. Tsetse flies were very active and poor Elsa found them most irritating, par-ticularly just after sunrise and again before sunset. She would rush frantically through the low bush to brush them off or would fling her itching body onto the ground, her normally sleek coat standing on end.

To make her more independent of our camp life we took her out for the whole day and, after an early morning walk of two or three hours, settled down in a shady place along the river. We picnicked and I took out my sketchbook. Elsa soon dozed off and I often used her as a pillow when I read or slept. George spent most of the time fishing and usually produced our lunch straight out of the river. Elsa had to have the first fish, but after mouthing it for a short time she would pull a grimace of disgust and show no further interest in the rest of George's catch. Nuru and the gun bearer proved to be excellent chefs and roasted our meal as soon as it had been caught.

Once we surprised a crocodile sunning itself on a rock; startled, it plunged into a narrow pool which was cut off by rapids at either end. The water was so clear and shallow that we could see the bottom, but we could see no sign of the "croc" and we wondered where it could have got to. We settled down to our meal; Elsa relaxed on the water's edge and I leant against her. Soon George got up to go on with his fishing; but first, to make sure that the croc was not still in the pool, he prodded along the bottom with a long stick; suddenly it was wrenched from his hand and a six-foot croc, which had been hiding in the sand, slithered over the rapids and disappeared into another pool. It had bitten off the end of the tough stick. As Elsa had not noticed this incident, and as we did not wish to encourage her to hunt crocodile, we moved away.

Shortly afterward a wart hog came along for his noonday drink. Elsa stalked him carefully, then, helped by a bullet from George's rifle, seized the pig by the throat and suffocated it. The encounter took place at a little distance from the river, and, as I thought it would be more comfortable for Elsa to guard her kill in the shade by the water, I pointed to the pig and then to the river, several times, saying: "*Maji*, Elsa, *maji*, Elsa." She was familiar with the word *maji*, which

Elsa dragged the pig into the river

I used when I wanted Nuru to fill her water bowl. Now it seemed that she perfectly understood this Swahili word for water, for she dragged her pig to the river. She played with the carcass in the water for nearly two hours, splashing and diving with it, and thoroughly enjoying herself until she was quite exhausted. Finally she pulled the pig onto the opposite bank and disappeared with it into a thicket; there she guarded it until it was time for us to return to camp, then she seemed determined not to be left behind, for as soon as we got up to go she dragged the kill back to our side. We cut it up before her and, having distributed the meat between Nuru and the gun bearer, set off with Elsa trotting good-naturedly behind us.

From then on, every time Elsa made a kill near the river she went to great pains to drag it down to the water and repeated the game she had had with the wart hog. We were at a loss to account for this strange behavior: perhaps she had accepted *"Maji, Elsa"* as a good rule and as part of her education.

These daily excursions brought all of us much closer together, and even Nuru and the gun bearer felt so much at ease in Elsa's presence that they did not bother to get up when she strolled over to them for a nose-rubbing or sat on them, in her playful way. Nor did they mind sharing the back of the Land Rover with her, and when she dumped her three hundred pounds between their bony legs they only laughed and petted her, while she licked their knees with her rough tongue.

Once, when we were resting on the riverbank with Elsa lying asleep between us, George noticed two black faces peering at us out of the undergrowth on the opposite bank. They were a couple of poachers armed with bows and poisoned arrows, who had chosen this spot to lie up and ambush game coming down to the water to drink.

Immediately he gave the alarm and dashed across the river closely followed by Nuru and the gun bearer; Elsa, suddenly alerted and always ready for a bit of fun, joined in the chase. The poachers made good their escape, but I would give a lot to hear the tale they had to tell when they got back to their village about how "bwana game"

As usual, Elsa drags a kill into the water (pp. 181-182)

(George's native name) was now employing lions to hunt poachers.

Early one morning when we were out on our pre-breakfast walk Elsa took the lead and with great determination headed in a set direction, toward a point at which we had heard much trumpeting of elephants during the night.

Suddenly she stopped sniffing the wind and, with her head stretched out, went off at a fast trot, leaving us behind. A few moments later, in the far distance, we heard the faint call of a lion. She stayed away all that day. Late in the evening we heard her call a long way off mingled with that of another lion. During the night hyenas were much in evidence and kept us awake with their inane laughter. At dawn we followed Elsa's spoor and soon found it leading away from camp and mixed up with the pugmarks of the other lion. The next day we found her spoor alone; on the fourth day of her absence we tracked her across the river. We searched for her all that day until we found ourselves unexpectedly in the middle of a herd of elephants; then there was nothing but to run for it. Early on the fifth morning Elsa returned very hungry and ate until her belly was near to bursting point. After that, she retired to my camp bed and made it clear that she was not to be disturbed. Later I noticed two deep bites and several smaller claw marks on the curve of her hind legs; these I dressed as best I could. She responded affectionately, sucking my thumbs and holding me close. In the afternoon she did not want to go for a walk and sat on the roof of the Land Rover until dark, then she disappeared into the night. Some two hours later we heard a lion's roar in the distance and Elsa's immediate reply. At first the sound came from near the camp, but gradually her voice faded away in the direction of the lion.

The following morning we decided that this was an opportune moment to leave her alone for another few days and moved camp so as not to handicap her association with the wild lion, who might take exception to our presence. We knew now that she was quite capable of looking after herself, which made this parting less painful than the first one, but I was worried about her bites, which looked as though they might turn septic.

After a week we returned to our camping place and interrupted Elsa while she was stalking two waterbuck. It was early in the afternoon and very hot; poor thing, she must have been very hungry to be hunting so late in the day. She gave us a touching welcome and gorged herself on the meat we had brought her. I noticed a new bite on her elbow and her old wounds were badly in need of dressing. For the next three days she made up for her period of starvation.

By now Elsa's fame had spread far and wide, and a party of American sportsmen paid us a visit specially to film her. She entertained them royally and did everything she could to please them. She climbed a tree, played in the river, hugged me, joined us for tea, and behaved in such a docile manner that none of our guests could believe that she was a full-grown lioness who shortly before they arrived had been equally at ease in the company of wild lions.

That night we heard a lion call, and Elsa promptly vanished into the darkness and was away for two days. During this time she returned for one brief visit to George's tent. She was most affectionate and nearly broke his camp bed by sitting on top of him as he lay asleep. After a short meal she went off again. In the morning we followed her spoor, which led us to a rocky ridge near the camp. After climbing to the top and looking unsuccessfully for her in all her favorite lying-up places, we nearly fell over her in a clump of thick bush. Obviously she had kept quiet in the hope that we should not see her. Yet, in spite of her obvious wish to be alone, she gave us her usual affectionate greeting and pretended to be very pleased to see us. We respected her feelings and tactfully left her alone. Late that evening we heard the roar of a lion and the howling of his retinue of hyenas upriver. Soon Elsa's voice sounded close to camp. Perhaps by now she had learned to keep away from her lord and master while he was at his kill and was waiting until he had his fill before making a closer acquaintance with him. Later she returned to George's tent for a few moments, put her paw affectionately around him, and moaned softly, as if to say to him: "You know that I love you, but I have a friend outside to whom I

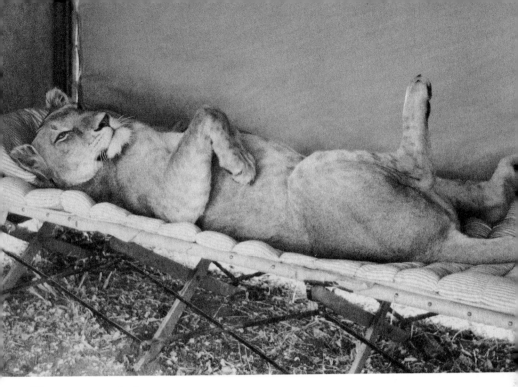

Elsa on a camp bed

simply *must* go; I hope you will understand," then she was off again. Early next morning we found the pugmarks of a big lion close to camp; obviously he had waited while Elsa went to George's tent to explain the situation. She kept away for three days, returning each evening for a few minutes just to show us her affection but going off again without touching the meat which was ready for her. When she returned after such escapades she always seemed more affectionate than ever, as though she wished to make up for having neglected us.

The rains had started, and as usual they stimulated Elsa's energy and playfulness. She just had to ambush us from any suitable cover. As among our pride I was her favorite "lioness," she honored me with most of her attentions, and so I was the one who usually found myself on the ground with Elsa's soft but heavy body on top of me, holding me down until George released me. Although I knew it was only affection that singled me out for these privileges, I had to stop this practice as I was quite unable to get her off me without help. Soon she understood by the tone of my voice that the game was not popular, and it was touching to see how she tried to control her pent-up energy so that, even when she was making a flying leap, she would control it at the last moment and reach me in a dignified manner.

After the first downpour of rain the dry, gray thornbush changed within a few days into a garden of Eden. Every grain of sand seemed to give way to a seed bursting up from beneath. We walked along tracks of luxuriant sap-green growth, each bush a giant bouquet of white, pink, or yellow blossom. But, however pleasing this transformation was to our senses, it only added to the anxieties of our walks, for now visibility was reduced to a few feet. There were rain pools everywhere and each was a concentration of freshly marked game tracks. Elsa took full advantage of these bush newsreels and would often leave us to go hunting. Sometimes we watched her stalking waterbuck, which she drove toward us, at others, followed her tracks while she was in pursuit of bushbuck; when doing this she would cleverly cut in a straight line across their winding tracks. However, as in these days she was well fed and had a full stomach, she regarded such hunts more as a pastime than as serious work.

One morning we were walking quietly along the river, intending to spend the day out; Elsa was with us, full of energy and, judging by the twitching of her tail, having a wonderful time. After walking for two hours we were looking for a place to have breakfast when, suddenly, I saw her stop abruptly, her ears cocked and her body tense with excitement. The next moment she was off, jumping noiselessly down the rocks which flank the river at this point; then she disappeared into the thick undergrowth below. Here the river is divided by several islets, each an impenetrable thicket of bush, fallen trees, and debris. We had stopped to wait for the outcome of her stalk when we heard, as I thought, the unmistakable sound of elephant trumpeting. Deep vibra-

George, Elsa, and Makedde

tions shook the air, and I was convinced that there was more than one elephant in the thicket below. George disagreed, saying that the noise was made by a buffalo. I had heard countless buffaloes making their various expressive bellows, but none had ever made such a typical elephant sound. We waited for at least five minutes, hoping that Elsa would get bored with her big friends as, after a short time, she usually did. Then came a deep rumbling sound, and before I realized what was happening George leapt down the rocks, saying that Elsa was in trouble. I followed, as fast as I could, but was brought to a halt by a fresh outburst of violent bellowings just ahead. I felt most uneasy as I penetrated the thick bush, imagining that at any moment the massive shape of an enraged elephant would break through and squash everything in its path. Instinctively the men and myself stopped and called to George not to go on, but nothing would deter him and he disappeared behind the green walls of creepers and trees. Now we heard an ear-splitting scream followed by urgent shouts from George: "Come, quick, quick!" My heart turned to lead—an accident must have happened. As I stumbled as fast as I could through the thicket, terrible scenes flashed through my mind. But soon, thank God, I saw George's sunburnt back through the foliage; he was standing upright, so all must be well.

Again he repeated his summons to hurry. When I finally broke through the bush to the riverbank, what I saw was Elsa dripping wet, sitting on top of a bull buffalo in the middle of the rapids. I could not believe my eyes; here was a buffalo helplessly forced down with his head half submerged, while Elsa tore away at its thick skin and attacked from every angle. We could only guess at what had happened since, ten minutes earlier, I first heard my "elephant noise." Elsa must have disturbed the buffalo—an old bull past his prime, as we later discovered —while he was resting close to the water, and chased him toward the river. Then in his attempt to cross he must have fallen on the slippery rock of the rapids; and Elsa had taken advantage of his predicament, jumped on him, and held his head under water until he was half drowned and too exhausted to get up. After this she had attacked him

Elsa and a buffalo (pp. 189-191)

at his most vulnerable spot, between the hind legs, and was doing so when we arrived.

George waited until Elsa gave him a chance to end the unfortunate animal's agony with a merciful bullet. As soon as this *coup de grâce* had been delivered, we saw Nuru wade, waist-deep, into the foaming rapids. He could not resist the chance of gorging himself on this mountain of meat, but, as he was a Mohammedan, he would not be able to eat the buffalo unless he had cut its throat before it died. There was no time to lose, so there he was venturing between the hidden, slippery rocks toward the kill. From her position on top of the buffalo Elsa

watched his every movement with tense excitement. Although she had known Nuru since she was a tiny cub and had allowed him every sort of familiarity, she was now highly suspicious and, with flattened ears and threatening growls, defended her buffalo even against her nanny. She looked really dangerous; but Nuru, driven by gluttonous visions, paid no heed to her warnings. It was a ludicrous sight to see his fragile skinny figure staggering fearlessly toward the fiercely growling lioness perched on the top of a dying and kicking buffalo; as he advanced he waved his first finger at her, calling out: "No, no."

Incredible as it may seem, Elsa obeyed him and, sitting quietly on top of the buffalo, allowed him to cut its throat.

The next problem was to get the dead beast out of the river. We had to drag it through the rapids between the slippery rocks. To achieve moving twelve hundred pounds in such circumstances, with an excited lioness guarding it, was no easy task.

But Elsa, intelligent as she is, soon realized what was required and by seizing him by the root of the tail, while three men pulled at the head and legs, literally helped to get the buffalo out. Combined with much laughter at Elsa's efforts, their joint strength succeeded in hauling out the carcass, which was then cut up. Here again, Elsa was most helpful. Each time one of the big, heavy legs was severed from the body she at once dragged it into the shade of a bush, thus saving the boys the task of doing so later on. Luckily, we were able to bring the Land Rover to within a mile of the scene and managed to get most of the meat to camp.

Elsa was exhausted: she must have swallowed quantities of water during her battle with the great beast, and she had spent at least two hours up to her neck in the fast current of the river. But, tired as she was, she would not leave her kill until she knew that it was safe and that all had been cut up; only when all was finished did she retire to the shade of a bush.

When I joined her a few moments later she licked my arm, embraced me with her paw, and hugged me to her wet body. We relaxed after the morning's excitement. I felt very touched by her gentleness and the care with which she treated my skin and avoided scratching me with claws that only a few minutes ago had been so deadly to the thick skin of a powerful buffalo.

Even for a wild lion, it would have been a remarkable achievement to kill a buffalo bull single-handed, let alone for Elsa, who had only recently learned the art of hunting from her very inferior foster parents. Although the river had been a good ally to her, it had needed considerable intelligence on her part to take advantage of it, and I felt very proud of her.

Late in the afternoon on our way back to camp, we came upon a giraffe drinking on the opposite bank of the river. Forgetting her weariness, Elsa stalked it; she crossed the river, most carefully, downwind and out of view of her quarry, and, avoiding making the least splash, she disappeared into the riverine bush. The giraffe, unaware of any danger, splayed its forelegs as far as possible, and bent its long neck down to the water to drink. We held our breath, expecting that at any moment Elsa would leap out of the bush and attack, but, to our great relief, the giraffe heard, or sensed, Elsa's presence in the nick of time and with a swift movement turned and galloped away. It was lucky for the giraffe that Elsa was so full of buffalo meat. Her adventures for the

Elsa on George's bed

day were not yet at an end, and as her motto seemed to be "The bigger the better," it only remained for an elephant to appear, ambling slowly along the game path toward us. While we hurriedly retreated in order to make a detour around him, Elsa sat quietly in the middle of the path and waited until the mighty animal was nearly upon her, then sprang nimbly aside, causing him to turn and make off at high speed. After this she quietly followed us back to camp, flung herself down on George's bed, and quickly went to sleep. Not a bad record for one day.

Not long afterward we were walking together along the shady riverbank when we noticed basin-shaped circular depressions of mud about three feet in diameter, in a shallow lagoon. George told me they were the breeding places of *tilapia*, a fish we had not so far seen in the river. While we investigated these mud hollows Elsa sniffed with great interest at a bush and wrinkled up her nose, a thing she often did when

Asleep

scenting a lion. Now we saw fresh pugmarks near by, and Elsa, who was purring distinctly, followed the spoor and disappeared. She kept away all night and the following day. When, in the afternoon, we looked for her, we detected her through field glasses outlined on her favorite rock. She must have seen us, for we heard her calling, but she made no attempt to move from her position. Thinking she might be near wild lions, we did not want to interfere, and returned home. After everyone had gone to bed George heard the agonized cries of an animal in pain, and after a short time Elsa appeared in the tent and threw herself down next to his bed. She patted him several times with her paws as though she wanted to tell him something. Then after a few minutes she left again and was absent all night and the following day.

While we were having our dinner next evening, she walked into the tent, rubbed her head affectionately against me, and then went out and spent the night away. In the morning we tracked her spoor over a long distance; it led far away. That evening she failed to come back; she had now kept away for three days, except for brief visits during which she had shown us her affection. Might this be her touching way of telling us that she had found her pride and, while she still loved us, was trying to loosen our ties?

During the night we were awakened by the most alarming lion growls mixed with the laughing of hyenas. We listened, expecting Elsa to come in at any moment, but morning dawned and she did not return. As soon as it became light we went in the direction from which the growls had come, but stopped after a few hundred yards, startled by an unmistakable lion grunt coming from the river below us. At the same time we saw an antelope and some vervet monkeys racing in flight through the bush. Creeping cautiously through thick under-growth down to the river, we found the fresh pugmarks of at least two or three lions in the sand; they led across the river. Wading through, we followed the still wet spoor up the opposite bank when I noticed, not fifty yards away, through the dense bush the shape of a lion. While I strained my eyes to see if it was Elsa, George called to her. She walked away from us. When George repeated his call she only trotted faster along the game path until we saw the black tuft on the end of her tail switch for the last time through the bush.

We looked at each other. Had she found her destiny? She must have heard us; by following the lions she had decided her future. Did this mean that our hopes for her to return to her natural life had been fulfilled? Had we succeeded in letting her part from us without hurting her?

We returned to camp alone, and very sad. Should we leave her now, and so close a very important chapter of our lives? George suggested that we should wait a few more days to make sure that Elsa had been accepted by the pride.

I went to my studio by the river and continued to write the story of Elsa, who had been with us until this morning. I was sad to be alone, but tried to make myself happy by imagining that at this very moment Elsa was rubbing her soft skin against another lion's skin and resting with him in the shade, as she had often rested here with me.

Postscripts

To us it seemed impossible, after more than three years of such close companionship, that we should lose all touch with Elsa, so long as she was willing to keep in touch with us.

As George, in the course of his duties, is constantly travelling, we have endeavored to pay a visit to the area where Elsa lives, at intervals of about three weeks. On arrival in camp we always fire a shot or two, or let off a thunder flash, and on nearly every occasion she has come running into camp within a few hours, giving us a great welcome and showing more affection than ever. Once it was fifteen hours before she came, and once thirty hours, when she must have been very far off and sensed our arrival in some mysterious way. During our three days' stay she never lets us out of her sight and is touchingly glad to be with us.

When the time comes for us to leave, George goes about ten miles away and shoots a buck or a wart hog as a farewell gift to Elsa while the tents are being struck and loaded up. In the meantime, I sit with her in my studio under the big tree and try to divert her mind. As soon as the buck arrives she has a good feed, though we usually find her fat and well. She obviously learned long ago to make her own kills and is quite independent of us for food. While she is eating, the loaded cars are taken about a mile away and, as she becomes drowsy after her meal, we sneak away.

For some time before the final parting she becomes noticeably aloof and turns her face away from us; although she wants desperately to be with us, yet, when she realizes we are going, she makes it easier in

Elsa and the author

this touching, dignified, and controlled way. As this happens every time, it can hardly be coincidence.

These were the last words I wrote before I came to England to arrange for the publication of Elsa's book. During the months I have spent in London, George has written me accounts of all his visits to Elsa, and her story is carried on by his letters. They prove not only her continued ability to combine the life of a wild lioness with her old relationship with us, but also that this relationship continues to be one of absolute equality quite different from that between a dog and his master.

Isiolo, March 5, 1959

After being delayed by the truck breaking down, and also my trailer again, I was able to get off to see Elsa on the evening of the 25th. Fifteen minutes after my arrival, Elsa appeared from across the river. She must have heard the diesel truck. She was looking fit, but thin and hungry. As usual, she made a great fuss of me before going to her meat. She was nothing like as thin as on the first occasion, and in a couple of days had put on flesh and looked as fit as ever. Obviously she was much puzzled that you were not there and went several times into your *boma*, and looked inside the truck, calling. However, she soon settled down into the usual routine, except that she absolutely refused to leave the camp for a walk. She would go to the studio in the morning and spend the whole day there with me. When I brought her the second buck on Sunday morning, she would not let anyone go near it and was quite fierce. But as soon as I went down to the studio she dragged the buck along, deposited it by my seat, and did not mind my cutting it up. In the afternoon when I went back to my tent, she picked up the buck and brought it along to the tent. The next afternoon I said: "Elsa, time to go home." She waited until I picked up the remains of the buck and then solemnly walked ahead to the tent. The white spots on her back had disappeared. Her friend the monitor was still there, waiting to steal what he could. Now, she seems to accept him and pays no attention when he comes to the meat. Still no sign of her contacting lions.

I left Elsa on Tuesday. I took particular care to keep her down at the studio while the camp was being packed up. But as soon as she heard the diesel go off, she knew at once that I was going to leave her and adopted the same aloof manner and would not look at me. I intend to go and see her again on the 14th.

Isiolo, March 19, 1959

I went again to visit Elsa on the 14th. Got away about 10:15 A.M. I arrived about 6:30 P.M.—there was no sign of Elsa, no spoor. I let off three thunder flashes during the course of the night, and a Very light. Next morning at dawn I set off to look for her. Went as far as the large water pool along the track where Elsa ambushed the elephant. The pool was dry, and no spoor of Elsa. I let off another thunder flash and returned along the top of the ridge to the car track, and then back to camp along the sand *lugga*[1] behind the camp. Still no signs. Got into camp about 9:15 A.M. A quarter of an hour later she suddenly appeared from across the river, looking very fit with plenty of flesh on her bones. She must have killed at least once since I left her eleven days before. She gave me a tremendous welcome. She had some scars, probably caused in the struggle with her last kill, but they were superficial and had hardly penetrated the skin. She settled down straight away to her usual routine. She was rather full of beans and twice knocked me over, once into a thornbush! She condescended to go out for a short walk down the river, but spent most of the days with me in the studio.

Still no signs of her being in contact with wild lions. I did not hear any on this trip. The country is very dry, which probably makes it easier for Elsa to hunt, as everything has to come to the river to drink and visibility is better. As I had only the mountain tent with me, it was a bit crowded at night with Elsa in it as well, but she behaved very well and never once wetted the ground sheet! As usual she would wake me up several times at night by "rubbing noses" and sitting on me. There was no trouble in leaving her, which I did on Wednesday. In fact, I think she is becoming more independent and does not mind being left alone. I really have no patience with people who maintain that an animal's life and actions are governed by pure instinct and conditioned reflexes. Nothing except reasoning powers can explain the

[1] Dry river bed.

200

Elsa and George

Elsa with George reading

careful strategy used by a pride of lions in hunting, and the many examples we have had from Elsa of intelligent and thought-out behavior.

Isiolo, April 4, 1959

I reached camp about 8 P.M. Let off the usual thunder flashes and a Very light. But there was no sign of Elsa and she did not appear during the night. Early next morning I went to the track where we shot the guinea fowl, and found the remains of a recent camp there. I then carried out a wide half-circle on the far side of the river, hoping to find her spoor, but saw no traces. By the time I got back to camp I was almost fearing that she had been shot.

I had arranged with Ken Smith to follow me, as he was very keen to see Elsa again. He was in camp when I got in and told me that he had seen Elsa on top of the big rock. He had called to her but she seemed nervous and would not come down. I went along with him, and as soon as I called and Elsa recognized my voice she came tearing down the rock and gave me a terrific welcome, and she was just as friendly to Ken. She looked the picture of health, her stomach bulging. She must have killed the previous night. Ken put his bed in your *boma* and Elsa did not worry him at all during the night. We even went out for a walk all together and spent the day in the studio, Elsa asleep on my bed and Ken on his, although she did sit on him once out of pure friendliness.

Thursday evening, Ken having left the previous day, I took Elsa up the rock. As I was thinking of returning to camp, a leopard started to grunt just below. Promptly Elsa went off to stalk it, but I think it must have heard me and gone off. I left her on Friday morning with a fat wart hog to keep her happy. Promptly she took it into the river and had a tremendous game with it. Elsa is now in quite perfect condition, no bones showing at all.

Isiolo, April 14, 1959

I had intended going to see Elsa yesterday, but I had to go and chase more elephants out of gardens. However, whatever happens I am setting off tomorrow. I can't tell you how much I always look forward to seeing her and her never-failing loving welcome. If only she could find herself a mate I would feel much happier about her. It must be very lonely for her. She must at times feel very frustrated, but it never seems to make any difference to her good nature and friendliness. What is touching is that she always knows when I am leaving her, yet accepts the fact and makes no attempt to interfere or to follow. In her dignified way she seems to know that it is unavoidable.

Isiolo, April 27, 1959

I set off to see Elsa on the afternoon of the 15th. Arrived about 8 P.M., nearly having run into two rhinos around a corner. Passed them a few feet off the track. I let off the usual thunder flashes and Very lights, but there was no sign of Elsa that night. Next morning I went to the rock and set off more flashes. No spoor to be seen anywhere. She did not turn up during the day or night. There was very heavy rain during the night with fantastic lightning and thunder and the river came down in flood. Next morning I walked to the "buffalo ridge" and down into the sand *lugga*, which had also been in flood, in fact, I had to leave it because of the quicksands. In one place I suddenly plunged up to my waist in sand and had quite a job getting out. I then followed the game path down a ridge to near a junction of the *lugga* with the river. Rather farther than we went before. Had lunch on the river-bank and then crossed over with the water waist-deep, and red with mud. Of course the rain had washed out any spoor there might have been, but anyway I followed the river back to camp.

At one place I saw an object in the water which I thought was the body of some dead animal. I went closer and was about to throw a stone at it when suddenly a head emerged and it was a hippo. Shortly afterward there was a tremendous snorting, grunting, and squealing in the bush alongside the path—a couple of rhinos making love! Reached camp about 5 P.M.—still no sign of Elsa! I was really very worried, as she had never before taken so long to appear. Forty-eight hours after I arrived, at about 8:30 P.M., I heard her low call across the river and a few moments later she came racing into camp, the picture of health and terribly pleased to see me. There was nothing to suggest that she might have been with other lions. She was hungry and finished off most of the hindquarters of the rather smelly *granti* I had shot on my way down. Next morning I went and got her a pig, which she much enjoyed. In fact she ate so much that she would not move out of camp.

On Sunday morning as we were in the studio—Elsa in deep sleep behind—I saw an eight-foot croc come out of the water onto the rocks opposite. I crawled to the edge of the river and took a movie shot and crept away to get my rifle from camp. Finally shot it through the neck. It never moved off the rocks. I sent Makedde over to tie a rope around its neck and then pulled it across. Elsa watched the proceedings with much interest, but still hadn't spotted the croc—not until it was close in to the bank. She approached it very carefully, just like the buffalo, put out a paw and tapped it on the nose cautiously, and then, satisfied it was dead, seized hold of it and brought it onto the bank, making a frightful grimace of disgust. She made no attempt to eat it, preferring the pig, which by now was very high.

I left Elsa on Monday morning; met a huge bull buffalo on one of the rain pools. The next morning went to hunt the big lion which we did not get the time Elsa's mother was shot. He has been giving a lot of trouble and eaten twelve of Roba's cattle during the last few weeks. Spent four nights sitting up over kills and part of the days looking along the rocky hills for his spoor. All I found was the spoor of a lioness with two cubs of about three or four months old—doubtless cousins or stepsisters of Elsa! Anyway I am not sorry the old lion did not turn up. I do not think he would be suitable for trapping, and taking to Elsa.

Isiolo, May 12, 1959

Well, I left on Sunday, May 3rd. As there had been very heavy rain during the week, I took only the Land Rover with Asman and Makedde. Got stuck in the same place where your car and my trailer became bogged and we had to spend the night out. Managed to get going again after about an hour's mud-larking and then became hopelessly bogged in the next *lugga*. Worked until dark without any progress. Camped the night. Heavy rain. *Lugga* in flood. Labored all morning, jacking up each wheel in turn, moving a few inches, and then down into the depths again. Finally by 2 P.M. managed to get across. Then came the next *lugga*, which was in high flood (the one where you insisted on ferrying stones in the Land Rover!). During the night a large pride of lions came and roared most of the hours of darkness close to camp. I think they had a kill near by. No rain, so after a bit of digging managed to make the crossing and went on and found the next river just fordable. It had been very high during the night. I went on.

Just before the turn-off to Elsa's camp, suddenly came on two rhinos in the middle of the track at about twenty-five yards. Mother and almost full-grown calf. As they showed no inclination to move, I got out of the car with my .303 rifle. The cow put its head down and charged. Halfway through the charge I shouted at her to bring her to her senses, but she merely accelerated and I was forced to fire. She spun around five yards from the bonnet of the car and made off. I followed up the spoor for several hundred yards, but there was no indication to show that she had been hit.

I then went on and made camp about 12:30 A.M. There were no signs of Elsa, and the river was in high flood, higher than we ever saw it. Naturally, any spoor there might have been was washed out by the rain. Let off thunder flashes and Very lights in the evening. Next morning still no Elsa. Went and followed the rhino spoor again for about two miles; no signs of blood or distress. Think I must have hit it in the horn. After looking for the rhino I went on and shot a gerenuk for Elsa, as the *granti* I had brought for her was stinking. Elsa did not turn up that day, nor the next two. I could not help feeling worried, although the most likely reason was that she had gone off with wild lions. I sent Makedde and Asman to make inquiries at the African settlements, but nothing had been heard or seen of any lions. So on Saturday morning with a heavy heart I started to pack up (I had been away a week already).

Suddenly there was a great uproar from the baboons across the river and in came Elsa dripping wet, looking as fit as ever. Her stomach was pretty empty, but she was not hungry as she turned up her nose at the gerenuk, for which I didn't blame her as it was stinking. She was the same old Elsa, full of affection and so pleased to see me. There was no indication that she had been with other lions, nor since you left has there been any sign of her being in season, but of course she may have been, in between visits. After she had settled down I went off and got her a fresh gerenuk. At night she brought it into the little mountain tent. As you can imagine, there was not much room for myself, Elsa, and the buck! However, as the buck was fresh I did not mind much, in spite of the blood and muck all over me and the tent.

Elsa has now been on her own for nearly six months. She is just as competent to look after herself as any wild lion and obviously goes off on long safaris, yet her friendliness and affection have not altered in the least degree and she is just the same as when you left. She is a wild lioness in every respect except one. And that is her extraordinary friendliness toward Europeans. I feel sure that she looks on us as some kind of lion, not to be feared and to be treated with ordinary casual friendliness. There is now no question of Elsa's waiting and pining for my return. She is always very pleased to see me and obviously does not like to see me leave her, but if I were to stay away for good, I do not think it would upset her life very much.

Isiolo, May 20, 1959

There is nothing more I can tell you about Elsa. I put every detail in my letters. You know when she is full of meat she will not go far from camp and just spends the days with me under the studio tree. Unless something unusual happens, it is the same routine as before you went away. Elsa is certainly more independent and goes farther afield and no longer has to rely on me for food. She is perhaps a little more suspicious of strange Africans and will not let Nuru or Makedde come too near when she is with her meat. When it comes to moving the meat, either from the tent to the studio in the morning or from the studio to the tent in the evening, I have to carry it with Elsa marching behind. Even in the little mountain tent, Elsa brings the meat into it and I just have to put up with it or, if it is too smelly, move my bed outside! Obviously she knows that when the meat is put near me it is quite safe. I feel sure that when she has cubs she will bring them along and deposit them with me to look after. When that happens I do not think it will be possible to have anyone near, apart from us. The staff will have to be left behind.

I look forward to seeing Elsa again. She was rather pathetic when I left her the last time. I tried to sneak away unseen, but when I looked back she was standing on the edge of the salt lick watching me go away. She never made any attempt to follow. I felt like a thief stealing away.

Isiolo, July 3, 1959

I managed to get away from Isiolo late on Saturday with an American doctor named Delaney and his hunter, Henry Poolman, to have a try for lions which it was reported had killed a Boran and mauled another. Delaney is a keen sportsman and wanted to hunt the lions himself. We reached our destination in the evening in a howling gale which created

George with Elsa

a dust storm over the flats. Next morning we went with a party of Boran to the place where the man had been killed. It is very dense bush. It seems that a party of about eight Boran went after seven lions which had killed a camel. They came on the lions, one of which —a male—showed fight. A Boran threw his spear and grazed its flank. The lion, thoroughly angry, lay in wait, and as soon as the Boran took up the spoor, it sprang on one of them and bit the man through the arm. The rest of the party rescued their wounded comrade and carried him out of the bush. Then they returned to the fray and located the lion in an absolutely impenetrable thicket. One man foolishly ventured in a few yards. Before anyone realized what was happening, the lion had got him, bit him in the chest, and then retreated again into his stronghold. The injured man was rescued, but died shortly after. We found fresh lion spoor and followed it some way into the bush, but as it was leading downwind I decided the best chance was to try to attract them to a bait and to sit up over it. I left Delaney and Poolman and went to see Elsa, reaching there about 8 P.M. A quarter of an hour after getting in, she appeared, and gave me the usual welcome. She looked fit but was very hungry, and during the night ate nearly half the Grant's gazelle I had brought her. Early next morning she dragged the remains into the bush below camp and stayed there the whole day, paying me a few visits at the studio just to make sure I was still there. On Tuesday morning, having finished her meat, she followed me downriver for half a mile. Suddenly she became very interested in the far bank, and had obviously scented something. Presently she very cautiously went upstream along the bank and crossed the river. I hid myself opposite the place she seemed so interested in and waited. I could neither see nor hear anything. Suddenly, there was a commotion and a male waterbuck burst out of the bush into the river and came straight toward me, with Elsa close on its heels. Seeing me, it tried to turn, but Elsa was on it and brought it down. There was a tremendous struggle in the water. Elsa quickly changed her grip and clamped on to its throat. Then, when its struggles had become feeble, she got it by the muzzle, enveloping the whole of the forepart of its face in her jaws, obviously with the idea of cutting off its breathing. At length, I could not stand the sight any longer and gave it a merciful bullet. The buck must have weighed a good four hundred pounds. With a tremendous effort Elsa dragged it halfway up the almost sheer bank, then seemed defeated. I tried to help her but could not move it. I left her and went back to camp to get Nuru and Makedde with ropes. When we returned, the buck was high and dry on top of the bank! Elsa's strength is incredible—imagine what she could do with a mere human, if she wanted? It just shows how forbearing and gentle she is with us. I left her on the 2nd, with much difficulty. She knew I was leaving, and for a long time watched me intently and would not let me out of her sight. Finally, after two hours she fell asleep and I was able to steal away.

Prepare yourself for a tremendous welcome! In fact, I think it would be best if you did not show yourself until after she has greeted me and settled down a little.

*

I arrived in Kenya on July 5th.[1] Before the aircraft landed at Nairobi Airport and long before I saw George, I saw our Land Rover; it was by far the most battered car among the shiny limousines in the parking place. However much I may have blushed at other times to be connected with such a shabby vehicle, I felt now deeply moved to see it standing there with all its scratches and dents where Elsa had left her marks. I suggested to George that we should start straight away to visit her, but he convinced me that we ought first to buy a new Land Rover, as our old friend was literally falling to pieces. And so we had to part with this good but decrepit companion which was so much part of Elsa, and bought the latest luxury model, which was of course much more comfortable and respectable. But we wondered how Elsa would react to it.

George had arranged his local leave to coincide with my return, and soon we were on our way to Elsa. When we arrived at her camp on July 12th, it was already getting dark. About twenty minutes later, while we were putting up my tent, we heard the well-known barking of baboons coming from the river; these always heralded Elsa's arrival.

George suggested that I should get into the truck until Elsa had used up a little of her energy in greeting him, as he was afraid that in her excitement at seeing me after such a long parting she might not be able to control her great strength and might do me some injury.

[1] *Publisher's Note.* Fortunately, it has been possible to include the following pages written by Mrs. Adamson since her return to Kenya.

211

Rather reluctantly I followed his advice and watched her welcome him, but after a few minutes I got out. Suddenly she saw me and, as though it were the most natural thing in the world, walked quietly over from George and started rubbing her face against my knees and miaowing in her usual way. Then, with claws well tucked in, she used her three hundred pounds to bowl me over, after which she played in her usual friendly way without any fuss or excitement. She has filled out and grown enormously, and I was glad to see that her stomach was full; owing to this it was a long time before she showed any interest in the Grant's gazelle which George had brought. To our surprise, later, she jumped onto the roof of the new, shiny Land Rover with the same matter-of-factness with which she had greeted me, though it looked so very different from the old battered vehicle she was used to.

For the night we decided that I would put my camp bed into my truck, in case Elsa might feel inclined to share it with me. This proved a wise precaution, for soon after the lamps were turned out she crept determinedly through the thorn fence which surrounded my *boma* and, standing on her hind legs, looked into the truck and satisfied herself that I was there. However, after this she settled down next to the car till early morning; then I heard her dragging the Grant's gazelle carcass down to the riverbank, where she guarded it until George got up and called for breakfast. Then she reappeared and was about to make a flying leap toward me; but when I called: "No, Elsa, no," she controlled herself and walked up quietly and, while we ate, sat with one paw touching me. Then she returned to her neglected kill.

For the next six days Elsa shared our camp routine and our morning and evening walks. One day we watched her stalk a waterbuck while he was drinking on the other side of the river. She froze rigid in a most uncomfortable attitude till he gave her a chance to move swiftly downwind, then, crossing the river without the slightest splash, disappeared in the bush. When she returned she rubbed her head against us as if to tell us about the obvious failure of her hunt. On another occasion we surprised a large bird of prey on the body of a freshly

Reunion: Elsa and the author

killed dik-dik; when it left its victim we offered this little antelope to Elsa but she refused it, wrinkling up her nose in her usual grimace at anything she does not like. Another time we picnicked downriver for a day's fishing and I sat making sketches of her. As soon as I started eating my sandwiches she insisted on getting her share and tried with her big paws to snatch them from my mouth.

At other moments she was not so gentle, and we had to be on the alert to avoid her playful ambushes, for she has become so strong now that the impact of her heavy body is certainly no mutual pleasure.

One morning she had a wonderful game in the river with a stick which George had thrown to her. She retrieved it, leapt in caprioles around it, splashing all the water she could whip up with her tail, dropped the stick again only to have an excuse to dive for it and bring

Elsa and George resting

it proudly to the surface. While George was filming her near the water's edge, she pretended not to notice him but cunningly maneuvered herself closer and closer; then she suddenly dropped the stick and leapt on the poor fellow as if to say: "That's for you, you photographer." When George tried to get his revenge, she hopped away and with unbelievable swiftness climbed a sloping tree trunk out of everyone's reach. There she sat, licking her paws, looking utterly innocent.

After this performance Elsa paid us only short visits for the next two days and became very detached. On the 23rd she did not come for our morning walk, but in the late afternoon we observed her outlined on the rock ridge near camp and could hardly believe our eyes when we saw a whole troop of baboons within twenty yards, apparently quite unconcerned. Very reluctantly she answered our call and joined us at the foot of the rock, but soon afterward walked away as fast as she could into the bush. We followed until it was dark. Later she came back to us and put up with my patting her but was obviously restless and uneasy and wanted to go off. All that night and the next day she was away, coming only once for a quick meal. The following day while we were talking after supper she suddenly appeared dripping wet from having crossed the river. She greeted George and me affectionately, but while eating her dinner she constantly stopped to listen to something outside. By morning she was gone. This strange behavior puzzled us. She showed no sign of being in season, and we began to wonder whether we had outstayed our welcome. This was far the longest we had spent with her since her release.

Next evening again at dinnertime Elsa suddenly appeared out of the darkness and with one swish of her tail swept everything off the table; after embracing us with rather excessive affection she went off into the night, though she returned for a brief moment as if to apologize.

Next morning the explanation for her strange behavior was written plain in the pugmarks of a large lion. In the afternoon we saw, through our field glasses, a lot of vultures circling and went to investigate; we found the spoors of many hyenas and jackals and the pugmarks of a lion. These led toward the river, where the lion had no doubt drunk and had left a large pool of blood-soaked sand. But there was no sign of Elsa's tracks and no kill to account either for the vultures or for the blood. We spent six hours searching the surrounding area but had to return to camp without solving the mystery. That evening Elsa came in very hungry and spent the night with us, but was gone by dawn.

On the 29th we saw her on the high rock ridge, and after a few minutes' calling she joined us, purring repeatedly and affectionately, but soon returned to her rock. Now we saw that she was in season, which explained her recent behavior. When we visited her again in the afternoon, although she replied to our calls, she would not come down and we had to climb up the rock. When it was getting dark she got up and as if saying good-bye to us rubbed her head against me, George, and the gun bearer and then walked slowly toward her lie-up. Only once did she look back at us. Next day I saw her through my field glasses resting on her rock. If she could have spoken she could hardly have told us more convincingly that she wanted to be left alone. However much affection we gave her, it was plain she needed the company of her own kind.

We decided to break camp. As our two cars passed below her rock, she appeared on the sky-line and watched us driving away.

Our next visit to Elsa was between the 18th and 23rd of August. She was as usual most affectionate while she was with us, but out of these five days she spent two alone in the bush and, although we did not see the spoor of a lion, she seemed to prefer solitude to sharing our life. It was of course best for her that she should become independent of our ties.

On the 29th of August George was obliged to go to Elsa's area for Game control and arrived at 6 P.M. at her camp to spend the night there. He fired off two thunder flashes to attrack her attention. At about 8 P.M. he heard a lion downriver and let off another thunder flash. The lion continued to call throughout the night, but there was no sign of Elsa. Next morning George found the pugmarks of a young lion or lioness close to camp. He had to leave immediately afterward but returned at 4 P.M. An hour later Elsa came across the river, looking very fit and full of affection. Although she was not hungry, she ate a little of the buck which George had brought her and then dragged the carcass into the tent. Soon after dark a lion began to call. Much to George's surprise, she completely ignored the invitation, which continued throughout most of the night.

Elsa swimming across the river

Early next morning she made a hearty meal and then without any show of hurry disappeared in the direction from which the lion had called. Shortly afterward George heard her voice and saw her sitting on a big rock and heard her making deep grunts. As soon as she spotted him, she came down and met him but, although pleased to see him, made it obvious that she wanted to be alone and after a brief head-rubbing disappeared into the bush. Guessing the direction she had taken, George followed and found her running tracks heading for the river. Presently he saw her sitting on a rock almost hidden by bush. He watched her for some time. She seemed very restless and kept on looking intently downstream. First she miaowed, then with a startled "whuff-whuff" dashed down the rock and streaked past George into the bush. Next moment a young lion appeared, evidently in hot pursuit, and not sensing George came straight toward him. When the lion was less than twenty yards away George thought it time to act and waved his arms and shouted. Startled, the beast spun around and made off the way he had come. A few seconds later Elsa reappeared, squatted nervously close to George for a few moments, and then followed the lion. George withdrew and moved camp.

Two days later he had to revisit the same area. A few hundred yards before reaching Elsa's camp one of the men in the car saw her under a bush close to the track, apparently hiding: most unusual behavior, for normally she would rush out to meet the car and greet everyone. Thinking the man might have mistaken a wild lioness for Elsa, George turned the car and drove back. There she was sitting under the bush. At first she made no movement; then, realizing that she had been caught out, she came forward and was courtesy itself, making a great fuss of George and pretending to be as pleased as ever at seeing him, and she condescended to eat some of the meat he had brought her. While she was eating, George walked up the track to look for spoor. He found her pugmarks together with those of another lion. Then he saw the lion himself peeping at him from behind a bush. It appeared to be the same one which he had seen with Elsa a few days earlier.

Presently there was an uproar from a troop of baboons by the river, which heralded the approach of the lion. Hearing this, Elsa hurriedly finished her meal and went off to find her lord and master.

George went on and pitched camp and left the remainder of the meat in the tent for Elsa, before going on to do his work. On his return to camp the meat was still untouched and Elsa did not appear during the night.

At last Elsa has found her mate, and perhaps our hopes will be fulfilled and one day she may walk into camp followed by a litter of strapping cubs.

Publisher's Note

As the culmination of this story, at the end of December we received the following cable:

CUBS BORN 20TH—ADAMSON

L'Envoi

W e have achieved our aim, at the cost of a bitter wrench to our-selves. Elsa is free; she has now lived the natural, independent life of a wild lioness for more than a year and yet retains all her affection for us, who nurtured her for so long. Who can tell how much further we may be permitted to follow her future career? We shall certainly try.

Whatever her ultimate fate may be, we shall always be thankful that she has given us a unique experience and the abiding memory of a most lovable character. If I have sadly to confess that "With a great sum obtained I this freedom" for her, I like to think that when she rubs her face against mine she is trying to comfort me by saying, in her own way,

But I was free born.